CREATIVE CASH

JAKE  GINO

— Present —

CREATIVE

CA$H

THE COMPLETE GUIDE TO MASTER LEASE OPTIONS AND SELLER FINANCING FOR INVESTING IN REAL ESTATE

BY BILL HAM

CREATIVE CASH

The Complete Guide to Master Lease Options and
Seller Financing for Investing in Real Estate

ISBN   978-1-5445-1857-2 *Paperback*
       978-1-5445-1856-5 *Ebook*
       978-1-5445-1858-9 *Audiobook*

This book is dedicated to my wife, Yvonne, who has been with me since the beginning of my real estate career. We met when she became my banker at my local bank in Macon, Georgia. I can honestly say she didn't start dating me for the money. She could literally see the account.

Special thanks to Julia Barbaro for her encouragement in my writing! If it wasn't for her personal coaching, I wouldn't have been able to sit still long enough to get this book written.

Jake and Gino, thank you for all your support. Couldn't have done it without you!

CONTENTS

FOREWORD 11

INTRODUCTION.............................. 15

1. COOPERATION 21

2. THE 3 PILLARS OF REAL ESTATE 27

3. BARRIERS TO ENTRY 39

4. UNDERSTANDING DISTRESSED ASSETS 45

5. SELLER FINANCING...................... 49

6. EQUITY PARTNERS VERSUS DEBT PARTNERS 61

7. MASTER LEASE OPTIONS 75

8. FINDING DEALS........................ 105

9. DEAL ANALYSIS....................... 127

10. MAKING OFFERS 167

11. DUE DILIGENCE...................... 179

12. NEGOTIATING THE DEAL 197

13. EXIT STRATEGIES................... 211

14. STEP-BY-STEP WALK-THROUGH.......... 221

CONCLUSION........................... 227

MORE FROM JAKE & GINO PUBLISHING 229

ABOUT THE AUTHOR 231

FOREWORD

It was a hot, sunny Saturday afternoon in Atlanta, and Jake and I were attending a real estate conference. I remember little about the conference, other than the air conditioning not working, but as fate would have it, I was introduced to an investor who lived in Atlanta. His name was Bill Ham, and although our paths had never crossed, I had heard his name mentioned several times in the real estate education space.

We had just written a best-selling book and were looking to scale our education company when we learned that Bill was interested in getting back into coaching and teaching. Over the next few weeks, we persuaded Bill to become our first real estate coach, and just like that, we became an education company with an accomplished coach.

Bill is an amazing coach with real-life experience, thousands of hours of coaching students, and a passion to help students excel in this competitive industry. What impresses me about Bill is his character, his dedication to his wife, his honesty, and the way he goes the extra mile for people while expecting nothing in return. His influence has allowed the community to thrive from a couple of hundred members to over thousands of active and engaged multifamily investors. It was Bill's credibility and experience that allowed us to grow and impact thousands of lives.

Over the next couple of years, I witnessed Bill teaching up close at our on-site boot camps and engaging with the community. His style of teaching is laid-back, yet his grasp of the subject matter is impressive, and Bill shines in his ability to teach the students challenging subject matter.

When Bill mentioned he had written a book on creative financing, I knew that this book could change lives. The topic of creative financing had become a lost art over the past few years due to the forces of an extremely hot real estate market, but I knew it was only a matter of time before the market reversed its course and creative financing would become more prevalent.

We had just published our second best-selling book, *The Honeybee*, and I knew how overwhelming it was to publish a book. I approached Bill and asked him if he wanted to rewrite his book and said we would help him publish it.

Thankfully, Bill thought it was a terrific idea, and we all got to work. I am extremely proud of the book that Bill has assembled. His writing is remarkably like his teaching: thoughtful, educational, entertaining, and full of real-life examples.

I am confident this book will shatter one of the biggest limiting barriers to entry in multifamily real estate, which is lack of money. Who better to write a book than Bill Ham, an investor who started out with no money and purchased his first four hundred units without ever stepping foot into a bank?

There are many real estate experts teaching out there but very few who have the results. What makes this book different is that Bill has been through the ups and downs of investing and, more importantly, is continuing his journey in real estate by utilizing the strategies you are about to embark upon.

Make It Happen!

Jake and Gino

INTRODUCTION

I can tell you everything you need to know in order to build a successful real estate business in one sentence. Here it is: Know the values of the assets in your market, and analyze more deals than anyone else.

That's it. Everything there is to know about real estate is contained in that sentence.

If you know the worth of the real estate deals in your market, you will know when a property is selling for a discount. If you look at more deals than your immediate competition (other investors), you are more likely to find properties selling at that discount.

It sounds simple, and it is, but building a business is never easy. It is simple, just not easy.

On average, you will close about 1 in 80 deals that you analyze if you use a traditional lender such as Freddie Mac (Federal Home Loan Mortgage Corporation), Fannie Mae (Federal National Mortgage Association), or local bank lenders. Finding properties to buy at a good price is simply a numbers game. If you look at enough deals, you will get about 1 of 80 to the closing table.

Creative financing is the art of increasing that number by creating problem-solving offers that don't rely on traditional lending.

You (the borrower), the property, and the market all factor into qualifying for a loan from a traditional lender. Sometimes properties are distressed or need work. Sometimes the borrower doesn't have enough down payment money, net worth, or credit to qualify for the purchase. Sometimes markets can decline, causing lenders to exit the area. Sometimes lenders don't feel like doing loans for unknown reasons.

Creative financing can help you create viable deals in any market cycle or lending environment.

Creative financing comes in many forms. There is the borrowing of private money to do deals. There are partnerships with sellers, Master Lease Options (MLOs), and seller financing. The possibilities are limited only by your imagination and ability to negotiate a problem-solving offer for a seller.

In this book, we'll focus on two primary forms of creative financing: seller financing and Master Lease Options. I have found these to be the two most common and effective ways to do real estate transactions creatively.

ABOUT ME

At the time of this writing (summer of 2020), I have been in the real estate business for 15 years. In that time, I've created a large portfolio of commercial real estate, consisting mostly of apartment complexes. I've built a management company with over sixteen employees, and I've operated all of the assets in my portfolio for the 15 years I have been in business.

I started with a duplex. By the time I quit my job as a corporate pilot in Macon, Georgia, I had $10,000 saved, and my duplex was cash flowing $300 a month (as long as nothing broke). A good friend had financed the deal for me for a short time. This allowed me to go to the bank, refinance the deal, and pay off the seller financing.

Over the next few years, I built a portfolio of 402 units, and I didn't receive a single loan from a traditional lender (such as a bank) to buy the deals. Not one. Every deal I did, I did with some form of problem-solving creative offer. As I solved my problems (no money and no experience), I found ways to solve each seller's individual problem.

In 2008, the US economy went into one of the worst recessions since the Great Depression. The real estate market became very depressed. Lending was exceedingly difficult to come by. After this time, however, I saw one of the best real estate markets on record.

I have been full cycle now. I've not only experienced both up and down market cycles; I've also survived them. I have seen markets where there were good deals everywhere but no money to buy them. I have seen markets where there was too much money available but no good deals to buy.

The market we have today will not be the market we are in tomorrow. What worked yesterday will not work tomorrow. As real estate entrepreneurs, we need to understand all market cycles, and we need to have strategies to make our business successful in both down and up markets.

ABOUT YOU

It's easy to make money when the market is rising and covering all mistakes, but can you be successful in a recession? Can you find deals when no one else can? Can you get them funded? I will show you not only how to survive but also how to thrive by matching your purchasing strategies with the market condition, regardless of the economy.

I personally guarantee this book will increase your chances of closing more real estate deals.

Now, I didn't say that you would close more deals; I said *your chances would increase*. Business is about probability, not possibility. Success is about probability, not possibility. Anything is possible...but is it probable? Some people call it luck. I call it creativity.

This book is about art of creative financing and using new techniques to solve real estate problems. You will learn step-by-step instructions in each chapter that will teach you the skills to identify valuable deals (that have been there the whole time).

With more real estate "tools in the toolbox," you will increase the chances of being able to make an offer that will solve a seller's problems. Solving problems is a good business to be in, and solving real estate problems is a great business to be in. Creativity is the key to cash flow.

If you are starting out in real estate investing, this book will teach you the craft of trading your time and energy (sweat equity) for a seller's real estate, using techniques such as seller financing and other creative strategies. Whether getting your first deal or adding to your portfolio, the creative deal structuring techniques in *Creative Cash* will get your business to the next level.

If you have already delved into real estate, you know that getting a great deal is the crux of the business. Creative financing can and will give you the ability to look at deals in a new light. Distressed assets that otherwise would not be financeable become cash cows! Real estate is hard work, but if you're willing to do what it takes to be successful, *Creative Cash* will take you the rest of the way.

CHAPTER 1

COOPERATION

To fully understand the art of obtaining creative and seller financing (CSF), you must first understand what money really is.

Money was invented to make trading easier. Instead of always having to trade goats and chickens, we created currency. Over the years, that currency has changed form from seashells to gold coins to paper, backed only by the confidence in our government (fiat currency). No matter what form money takes, it has always represented one thing: *cooperation*.

If two people are unwilling to cooperate or trade with each other, money has no value. If you are alone on a deserted island with $1,000,000 in cash, it has no value. The money only has value when someone else agrees that it does. By itself, it's actually worthless.

This is not a hard concept to understand, but it reveals something important. If you remove money from a deal, you are just *cooperating* with others. You simply use money to facilitate that cooperation.

Let's work backward for a minute. What are you trying to do in real estate? Buy good deals that make money. What does it take to buy those good deals? Money! So what if you don't have any money?

If it takes money to do business and you don't have any money to get started, then you have to fall back on the one thing you have and can create: cooperation. If money is cooperation at its core and you can create cooperation with people who have what you want (sellers), do you need money to get started?

NO!

All of the real estate in America (and in most countries) is already owned or controlled by someone else. There are no more "land rushes" where settlers can run out, stick a flag in the ground, and claim that land. Someone already owns it. The trick is to get the people who already own the land and properties to give them to you.

This is where cooperation comes in. If you have all the cash in a checking account to buy all the property you'd ever want, then you probably don't need to read this book. But you do know who has what you want (sellers) and that you don't have to spend cash to get what you want (properties). So it's time to create cooperation.

START WITH PROBLEMS

There's one thing that is common among all people:

Problems!

It doesn't matter if you are rich or poor. It doesn't matter if you are just starting in the real estate game, or if you have been here for years. Chances are, you have problems. See where I'm going with this? The people who have the deals you want to buy are likely to have problems, too. If you can find ways to solve problems for these sellers, then you will create cooperation. Remember this simple equation:

Cooperation = Cash

If a seller owns one of those 79 "other" deals that is not good, then chances are, they have problems. At the very least, they probably can't get someone to buy their property at the moment. They may have occupancy problems. They may have repairs that haven't been done for a while. They may not be able to manage the asset anymore. They may be a "burned-out" landlord.

If you can solve the seller's problems by creating cooperation, then you don't need to be rich to start in the real estate business. CSF is based around creating value through problem solving.

Problems = Areas of Opportunity

You must start with the right attitude toward getting the business. Then you can use specific techniques to solve people's real estate problems.

There are a few easy ways to identify problems in your market. These problems are seller problems as well as investor problems. In the chapters that follow, I will show you how to create solutions to these problems that result in creative financing.

Sellers and local investors are the greatest source of CSF. Here is a list of problems to look for in your markets.

WHEN WORKING WITH SELLERS

1. Distressed assets
   A. Deferred maintenance
   B. Low occupancy
   C. Bad management
2. Burned-out landlord
   A. Tired of dealing with current management (bad management)
   B. Tired of spending money on the property
   C. "Accidental" landlord. Some people inherit property and don't really want to be in the business.
3. Cannot find qualified buyers
   A. This can be a real problem in a down cycle for most sellers. Many buyers have exited the business or are waiting on the sidelines to get back in during an up cycle.
   B. Look for sellers who've had a deal fall out of contract more than once. These sellers will be motivated and educated on the lower value of their property.
4. Taxes!
   A. Creative financing can be a way for sellers to mitigate tax liabilities. If a seller finances a deal to you, they will pay taxes only on the profit they receive. This is usually the interest you pay them for financing. Get with an accountant to verify any tax mitigation plan before making an offer.

WHEN WORKING WITH INVESTORS:

1. Getting low returns on current investments
2. IRA/401(k) giving low returns
3. Don't know how to invest in real estate
4. Don't have a real estate education
5. Can't manage or run a property but want to be in the business
6. Don't have the time to find good deals
7. Unaware that there are people who want to borrow their money and give them higher rates of interest
8. Unaware that real estate provides great tax benefits

I built my entire portfolio on the single concept of creating value by solving problems. I started with almost nothing in a bad neighborhood. I clawed my way out of that area by creating more and more value through real estate problem solving. I found sellers and investors who needed my services, and I was rewarded within my portfolio and the income that it produced. I never had a job after that and have been my own boss ever since.

What I'm suggesting is not easy. What I'm going to teach you will take a lot of work. You will need to be prepared to bring a lot of "sweat equity" to the table when dealing with sellers and properties. Some people want the secrets to getting rich quickly. I hate to disappoint, but you will not find them here. What I'm going to teach you is how to build a real estate portfolio with as little risk and money out of your pocket as possible.

POINTS TO REMEMBER

Find sellers with problems. Figure out how to solve those

problems. Some of the best deals I have ever done were not distressed assets at all; they were just with distressed sellers. For whatever reason, they were motivated to sell. Usually, they were tired of dealing with the asset because they never got a proper real estate education.

Cooperation is the key to creating wealth. Find out what you need and want. Find out who has it, and then figure out how you can be valuable to that person. This is the art of creating money through cooperation.

ACTION ITEMS

Decide what value you bring to a seller. Make a list of all the values you could bring to a seller.

Find all the multifamily meetings in your area. Go to them. If there are no multifamily meetings in your area, then start with your local real estate investment association (REIA). These can be found online. Most REIA groups focus on single-family investing and not multifamily, but this is a great place to start looking for owners of smaller assets who may be motivated to sell.

CHAPTER 2

THE 3 PILLARS OF REAL ESTATE

Before you can be effective with creative financing, you need to have a full understanding of the 3 Pillars of Real Estate: *market cycle*, *debt*, and *exit strategy*.

If you understand the 3 Pillars, you will mitigate a vast majority of the risk involved with real estate investing. If you don't understand these concepts, you will likely make lots of money in real estate and then turn around and lose most of it during the next shift in the market. By understanding these concepts, you will not only make more money but also keep it!

I cannot stress enough the value of these Pillars. If you don't understand the concepts of market cycles and how to maximize your strategies, your business will be built on nothing but luck, and luck will never replace skill. It is good to be lucky, but depending on luck isn't a solid investment strategy.

MARKET CYCLES

Markets go up, and markets go down. Prices go up; prices go

down. What most people don't realize is that market shifts are quite predictable.

Keep in mind that all markets cycle—the real estate market, the stock market, apartments, offices, single-family homes. These are all individual markets and will have their own cycles independent of, and sometimes in sync with, the national economy. Understanding past market conditions will allow us to deploy the most accurate business model in the present.

DEBT

Without an understanding of debt (traditional or creative), the investor is likely to underwrite a deal incorrectly or to accept a loan from a lender that may be counterproductive to the exit strategy.

Most traditional commercial loans come with a prepayment penalty if you pay the loan off early. What if your exit strategy is to renovate the property and sell it for a large profit in a short amount of time? What if you fix up your property and want to refinance to pull out cash? If you get the wrong loan, you may see a fair amount of profit absorbed by the prepayment penalty. This is just one example of debt and its correlation to your business model.

EXIT STRATEGY

The exit strategy is the first part of any good real estate analysis and arguably the most important of the 3 Pillars. You must know the way out before you go in.

How can you tell if a deal is a good one or not if you don't know what you are going to do with it? Renovate and sell? Renovate and refinance? Hold forever and cash flow? These are a few exit strategies. For your analysis to be accurate, you need to know what the exit strategy is before you even consider making an offer.

THE 3 PILLARS TOGETHER

To have real staying power in the real estate business, you must fully understand and be able to implement the 3 Pillars in any market situation. Misunderstanding or misapplying one of these concepts can cost you fortunes.

With almost 8 years in the business, I made one of the costliest mistakes of my career. I lost over $1,000,000 on a deal because I didn't understand these pillars. Yes, one million dollars! I will share more about that story, but first, in order for you to see how I made such a devastating mistake, I need to show you exactly how these 3 Pillars work together.

To begin, you first need to understand the market cycle you are in and where the market is headed in the next 2–5 years.

UNDERSTANDING COMMON MARKET CYCLES

No one has a crystal ball, but you can follow a common pattern to maximize your real estate profits. The average real estate cycle lasts 8–10 years from top to top or bottom to bottom. If you are in a great economy now, you should reasonably expect an economic downturn in 2–4 years. If you are in a down cycle and prices are low, buy everything! The market will recover in 2–3 years, and your assets will rise in value.

Below are two examples of common market cycles:

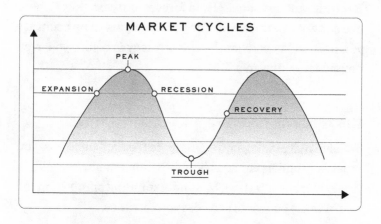

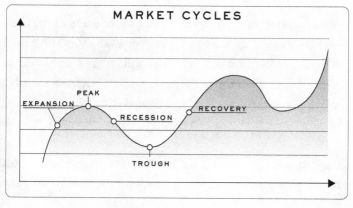

Figure 1 shows the market cycle in five stages: *expansion, peak, recession, trough,* and *recovery.*

Expansion is the time in the economy when we recover from a previous recession or decline. Jobs trend positive and wages are on the rise. Rent, interest rates, and loans all increase as well. In this economy, real estate prices are on the rise in most areas. Life is good.

The *peak* is the top of the market. Buying and pricing reaches a frenzied crescendo here. "We Buy Houses" signs pop up at every intersection. The market is on fire, and stories of quick riches in real estate abound. In this economy, properties are traded quickly and often off market.

Recession is just like it sounds. It's a downturn in the economy when pricing falls. Job rates slow and wage rates stagnate. Sellers who overpaid or overleveraged at the peak become exposed to new risks here. Some will become motivated sellers. By "motivated" I mean that for whatever reason, they will be ready to sell at a discount due to their pressing need. They have a problem. A building that needs a lot of immediate repairs would be an example. Recessions are great times for creative solutions to real estate problems.

During the *trough*, prices will be low, rents will be low, and the economy will be in bad shape. Lenders will be conservative, and lending will be scarce. The market is terrible during this time, and everyone says "you're crazy" for being in the real estate business. But you should buy it all!

The *recovery* is the upswing of the market. Unemployment is on the decline. Wage growth in the market increases. Prices are just starting to recover from the recession, and lenders loosen their criteria. This is the "fix and flip" market. Time to buy and renovate for big profits!

By understanding market cycles, you can apply the correct buying and exit strategies in each segment of the cycle. You will know what to avoid and what opportunities exist. For example, you don't want to refinance a property and pull out a ton of cash in the middle of a recession. Instead, you want to hold for cash flow and sell when the market recovers.

Making money is easy; keeping it is the trick. Who cares how much money you make in a great market if you turn around and lose it all in the next down cycle? As an investor and real estate entrepreneur, your staying power in this business is based on your ability to create profit by shifting tactics with the market cycles.

Figure 1 shows what a market looks like in theory. This chart shows that prices go from 1 at the beginning of the expansion to 100 at the peak, then back down to 1 at the next recession, only to rise to 100 again. Of course, no market operates exactly like this.

Figure 2 shows a more accurate depiction of the pricing in a market over time. Prices rise in the expansion and level off for a while at the peak. Pricing remains flat for a period of months and eventually declines. This decline is never a 100 percent drop. The level of price decline in a market typically depends on population growth and job growth (or lack of). At some point, prices will level off. Prices will remain flat for a few months, only to rise and level off at a new high.

DECIDE ON AN EXIT STRATEGY

Once you learn to analyze a deal by understanding which market cycle you are in, you can then figure out which part of the cycle you will likely be in when you own and ultimately exit the deal.

So what is your exit strategy? Are you going to fix and flip the asset? How long will it take you to fix it up? Will you lease for stabilization? Are you planning on refinancing or selling when you have completed your operational strategy? How long will it take to refinance? How long will it take to sell?

These are some questions you need to think about when you consider your plans for the property and how you will exit the deal. Depending on the extent of your renovations or "value add" business plan, you will need to decide how long it will take to reach the exit. How long do you plan to be in an operational mode with this deal?

Consider which part of the market cycle you will be in at the time of your proposed exit strategy. Does your exit plan match the market cycle? For example, if you are planning to renovate a property, you wouldn't do that during a declining market because the values will be dropping in your area. You might "catch the falling knife" or buy something just to see the value decline shortly after. Wait until the recovery cycle to carry out this strategy so you can maximize profits.

If your exit strategy is to sell or refinance, the appraisal of the property and its net operating income (NOI) will play major roles. Keep in mind that prices/appraisals will be at their lowest in the trough cycle. This is a great time to buy but not to refinance. Ideally, you want to hold and operate your property through the down cycle and sell or refinance in the upside of the expansion cycle, just before a peak.

ADD DEBT TO THE EQUATION

Now that you can see the importance of market cycles and exit strategies, you need to add debt to your business model.

During your initial analysis of the deal, you will decide on a hold time. You need to make sure you get debt that complements the time period. For example, if you plan to hold a property for 10 years and you have a loan that comes due in 7, you will have a forced exit strategy. Your loan will make you a motivated seller one day. You don't want to be in that situation.

If you use a "Fannie or Freddie" loan (Federal National Mortgage Association or Federal Home Loan Mortgage Corporation) that is set for 10 years, it will have a lower interest rate than other common market rate loans, but it comes with a big prepayment penalty (defeasance or yield maintenance) if you pay it off early.

This type of loan may seem attractive in rates and terms, but if you plan to renovate a property and sell or refinance it in a few years, it may be incredibly expensive to exit early. You may lose a fair amount of your profit or refinance proceeds to the lender.

If you plan to hold long term, get long-term debt. If you plan to hold short term, get short-term debt. This may seem like common sense, but many real estate investors always go for long-term debt. Why? Because short-term debt can seem expensive when considering interest rates and terms alone. But when you add in market cycles and your exit strategy, you can't value debt by terms and rates alone. You also must consider ease of exit from the loan.

So you want to get debt that matches your hold time while also considering the market cycle for your exit. Don't get short-term debt that will come due in a down cycle unless you have a very solid exit strategy and you are well capitalized. If you are currently at the peak cycle and you get a 3-year loan, your debt will likely come due during the trough, when prices and values are low. This is a poor exit strategy. If you're at the peak, you want to buy stable assets you can hold on to for 7–10 years. And you want to get long-term debt that won't come due in the trough.

So if you are currently in the trough, don't get long-term debt. Prices will rise in the next few years, and your opportunities to refinance or sell will be greatly improved by the market, if you don't have too much of a prepayment penalty on your loans. This is the time to fix up your properties and get ready to flip. This is another form of creative financing!

The trick is to be able to predict the market perfectly. How do you know exactly when a market has peaked? The short answer: You look back over our shoulder and say, "Oh, there it goes!"

No one knows exactly when and what a market will do. If they say otherwise, they are lying, selling you something, or just plain wrong. However, we can get good at predicting upcoming market cycles by studying the cycle we are in now and by looking at the most recent cycle. Through the lens of the 3 Pillars, the picture will become much clearer.

LEARNING THE 3 PILLARS THE HARD WAY

I created my first multifamily portfolio with creative financing in the post-2008 recession market. I created a second portfolio with traditional financing. In both cases, I made and lost money. In retrospect, 97 percent of the mistakes I made were a result of not following the advice I gave you above.

In 2008, I purchased a small apartment portfolio with a 3-year loan from a local bank. The loan came due in 2012, and the lender had not recovered well from the 2008 crash. In turn, my exit strategy was "motivated." Had I completed a 7- to 10-year loan at purchase, my debt would not have come due in a down cycle, and my exit would have been more profitable.

In 2015, I bought a larger portfolio of several hundred units with a long-term, fixed-rate loan from Fannie Mae. At the time, I believed we were near the peak of the market, but I was wrong. Within 2 years of purchase, I was selling. I chose the market due to a boon in job growth for the area. A large, local employer was expanding their operations near this property, and I knew this would create job growth. The decision made sense, but I didn't consider how quickly the market would rise. The property went up almost $20,000 per apartment in less than 2 years. I sold.

In total, I spent over $1,000,000 in prepayment penalties. That hurt. The returns on the deal were still great, but that prepayment stung. You bet I hated giving all that profit from my deal to the lender—just because we sold early.

What had I done wrong? I chose the right area, but I was off when it came to market cycles and debt. I mitigated risk by buying a good asset I wouldn't have to sell for 10 years if I didn't want to, but I had long-term debt. I was ready for a downturn in the market, but the downturn didn't happen. After that experience, I made sure never to get debt that would force a potential exit in a trough market.

POINTS TO REMEMBER

Creative financing relies on all 3 Pillars. In order for you to make creative offers that get accepted, you must be able to accurately analyze a deal and create a problem-solving offer. You can't do this if you have no understanding of the market cycles, what type of exit strategy you plan to employ, and how debt is part of your business plan. You could get a great deal with seller financing, only to have the seller's loan come due at the wrong time of the market and lose money. You could do a Master Lease Option deal in an upswinging market, but if you haven't considered all 3 Pillars you will likely still lose money.

Market cycles are a simple fact of business and economics. People might have opinions on how long each cycle will last and how high or low each market will get, but the existence of the cycles is irrefutable. The difference between a real estate investor and a real estate speculator is that the investor understands and utilizes the market cycles. The speculator makes money when the market is on the rise and usually loses it all when the market declines. To be successful in real estate over a long period, you need to understand market cycles and how to shift tactics based on upcoming market conditions. Anything else is real estate gambling, not real estate investing.

National and local market cycles may not always be in sync. Just because the national economy may be down, it doesn't mean every city and neighborhood is also in decline. Find the areas that are outperforming the national market.

Keep in mind the reverse can be true, too. I don't find the old adage "The rising tide floats all boats" to always be true.

I have seen many cities and some neighborhoods show a sharp economic decline, even when the national economy was reaching new heights in 2017 and 2018.

ACTION ITEMS

Prove it to yourself. Do some research on the topic of market cycles for real estate and business. This single topic could fill volumes of books. One specific way to continue your education on this subject is by looking at the pattern of post-recessions over the last 100 years. You will notice the rise and fall in the economy and see how it matches the market cycle charts.

When you are ready to invest in a deal, ask yourself these questions:

> ➤ What market cycle are we in now (nationally)?
> ➤ Are the local market cycles in sync (or not) with the national economy?
> ➤ What market cycle will we be in over the next 3–5 years?
> ➤ How does that affect my exit strategy and what I will choose when it comes to debt?

CHAPTER 3

BARRIERS TO ENTRY

You will face barriers to entry in the real estate business. The good news is that you can overcome these barriers.

MAJOR BARRIERS

LENDING

The appetite for lending comes and goes. Terms rise and fall with the strength of the market. When it comes to debt, there's plenty of money to buy deals when there are no good deals, and money is hard to find when there are lots of deals to be had.

In a good economy, everyone is buying. Therefore, the prices are high, and deals are difficult to find. Lenders are willing to lend, but returns on deals are low. In a bad economy, prices are low, making it a great time to buy. The problem is, lenders and investors aren't as willing to back real estate during that part of the market cycle.

QUALIFYING FOR A LOAN

To qualify for a loan, the borrower usually needs to have at least the same amount of net worth as the loan amount. In many cases, net worth needs to be 1.3 times the loan amount.

So if I want to qualify for a $1,000,000 loan to buy an apartment complex, then I need to show the bank at least $1,000,000 in net worth—possibly $1.3 million. The net worth for the loan can also be a collection of your net worth plus your partner's net worth, but in this case, you'd need millionaire partners to sign on the dotted line.

EXPERIENCE

Lenders and financial partners usually want to see that you already have some experience in the business you're trying to get into. If you're trying to buy single-family homes, you can probably do a few deals before lenders want to see your experience, but the income qualifications for the loan will be based off your personal income. Unless you're already rich, you'll be able to do only a few houses, and eventually you won't qualify for more lending based on your income.

If you are trying to get into larger multifamily properties (20+ units), then your experience will begin to come into question. If you haven't already done several of these deals, then the lender will want you to have a real estate résumé before they do business with you. This is similar to building credit when you are young. It takes credit to get credit, and without credit, it's almost impossible to find someone to give you any. It seems like an unfair catch-22. How do you get experience when no one will give you a chance?

FINDING GOOD DEALS

Finding good deals that have cash flow and can be purchased at a good price is a challenge in any market. Let's be honest here: if deals were easy to find and fund, you probably wouldn't be reading this book.

Most deals require a lot of repairs to be viable, or they are distressed in some other manner (such as low occupancy). In my *experience*, about 1 in 80 deals is good right off the shelf. Most are not. Most don't have cash flow, need a lot of work, or are simply overpriced.

Note: At this point, I suggest you call a mortgage broker or lender to verify the loan criteria I have suggested above. The lending environment changes all the time, and it's a good idea to stay in regular contact with your lenders and mortgage brokers. This will help you stay current on what it takes to complete loans in your area. Give them a call if you disagree with me or need an update on the lending environment.

THE SOLUTION: CREATIVE FINANCING

Seller and creative financing can be the solution to all these problems. In the rest of this book, you'll learn how to make this concept a reality for your business.

By mastering the art of creative financing, you will eliminate the need for traditional financing when getting started. In most cases, you will be able to take control of a deal and then refinance with a traditional lender or bank as an exit strategy if you choose. In some cases, you'll be able to secure private lending or seller financing that may allow you to hold and operate your property without ever getting a bank involved.

With creative financing, doing business with banks and traditional lenders becomes a choice, not a necessity.

Getting deals done creatively keeps you from having to qualify for a bank loan. If a seller gives you financing, then you are qualified by the fact they accepted your offer. If the seller doesn't think you are qualified, you will know as soon as they decline the offer. You can move on instantly, with no waiting or fees involved. You don't need a senior loan officer's approval.

Your experience in the real estate business will not be nearly as important when you do creative financing. Why? Because you will be solving real estate problems, and that's what sellers focus on. What's important is whether you can help them, not what your net worth is or how many units you already own. If you can help, you'll get paid!

Again, about one in eighty deals or properties is a good purchase just the way they are. With no work needed, it cash flows and will qualify for a bank loan. If you've been looking at properties, I'm probably just confirming something you already know. It's hard to find good deals!

How does creative financing address this problem? It adds tools to your real estate toolbox. The techniques I'll share will help you make more offers than you could before. You will be able to identify, analyze, and make offers on many more properties. You will increase your closing ratios by including deals that other people don't see as valuable. Distressed assets can be real estate "diamonds in the rough."

Above all, creative financing will help you get started in the real estate business and begin your path to personal freedom and wealth.

POINTS TO REMEMBER

It doesn't matter how much you start with. The only thing that matters is what you do with what you have. Everyone has a different starting point in business. Don't worry about it—just get started. Don't let barriers to entering a market stop you. Find a way.

There are always real estate deals in the world if you know how to look for them. No matter what market cycle you are currently in, there are deals to be had. There will not only be barriers to entry in all market cycles but also creative ways around each one.

ACTION ITEMS

Now is a good time to go to the bank and get a financial health checkup. You might be surprised by the fact that you can qualify for more (or less) of a loan than you previously thought. You can start this process by setting an appointment with three commercial lenders in your local market. The bank you use for your regular banking needs is a great place to start.

The purpose of these meetings is for you to sit down with commercial lenders and have them give you an idea of how much you can borrow to buy commercial real estate. Once you know this amount, you will be better prepared to make creative offers because you'll know how much real estate you can buy without creative financing.

Be prepared to bring your personal financial statements to these meetings. Be prepared to discuss your net worth, income, and real estate experience. But don't worry if you don't have a balance sheet or experience. Just go meet the lenders and start the conversation. It's free.

CHAPTER 4

UNDERSTANDING DISTRESSED ASSETS

There are a few things to keep in mind when considering CSF. The first is that you will likely be dealing with a distressed asset.

I have already mentioned this, but it's important and worth covering in detail. If a property is up and running and making tons of money, why would sellers finance it to you? They probably wouldn't. They would just sell it on the open market to a qualified buyer.

So you need to find deals where you can create value for the owners and for the property. This can be done by solving problems. So you actually *want* to look for distressed assets. The term "distressed asset" can refer to many things including:

1. Deferred maintenance
2. Low occupancy
3. Bad management

4. Units that need to be rehabbed (multifamily)
5. Bad tenant base (large number of nonpaying tenants)
6. Exterior building damage

These are common areas of distress I have encountered while building my portfolio. It's worth mentioning that in all the real estate I've dealt with, I've never done a deal that didn't have some level of distress or upside (the ability to raise its value through renovations) to it. When you can get a property at the right price with the right debt, renovating real estate can be extremely lucrative.

INCREASING MY NET WORTH BY $500,000 WITH A DISTRESSED ASSET

In January of 2010, I bought a 27-unit apartment complex for $240,000 (all with private money). Four units were occupied when I took over, and the property needed about $300,000 for total rehab costs. The day after I completed the repairs, the property was appraised for $500,000 more than I had invested in the project. I had used some creative ways to get the renovations done, too. (More on that in chapter 8.)

My net worth increased by $500,000 because I was willing to do this project with someone else's money. Then I refinanced at a bank and returned money to my financial backers plus interest. I will give details about this technique later in the book, but for now, I want you to realize the power of dealing with a distressed asset while leveraging creative financing. You can create tremendous wealth through "rehab" projects. Doing these projects with other people's money also helps to mitigate the risk.

Important Note: Attitude is everything. You must remember, the seller allowed their property to become distressed, not you. You bring a solution to the problem. They should be willing to bring the property to the table if you are willing to do the work.

POINTS TO REMEMBER

You can renovate a property but not an entire neighborhood. When dealing with distressed assets, look for the worst building on the block. You can simply bring it up to the standard conditions of the area. On the other hand, if you have the nicest building on the block, it will usually decline to match the rest of the area.

Look for distressed buildings that need minor renovations, not ones that have large structural issues. Also keep in mind the more distressed an asset is, the larger the opportunity costs. You can do only so many deals at once. You can manage only so much business or work at one time. If you plan to do a large renovation, consider the opportunity cost. How long will you be tied up with this project? How much money will be tied up and for how long?

If you do a large renovation project, make sure it's a good one because it will likely cause you to pass on other smaller deals that may come along. That's how opportunity cost works.

ACTION ITEMS

Go "windshield" a few deals. Drive by a deal and quickly take a look. I suggest driving around your market and pulling into a few apartment complexes. Don't get out and engage tenants, as that may anger owners or management. Just drive through the parking lot and look at the exterior of the buildings.

What do you see? How does the asset look and feel? How do the roofs and siding look? Do you see rotten wood or other signs of distress? This is a good way to practice looking at multifamily assets before you start reaching out to sellers or agents.

CHAPTER 5

SELLER FINANCING

Seller financing is my favorite form of creative financing. Seller financing is exactly what it sounds like. The seller or owner of a property will finance the deal for you, just like a bank or traditional lender. This means you will need to impress the seller enough for them to give you the financing, but you won't need to qualify with a traditional lender.

If a seller is openly advertising seller financing, be careful. The property is likely in unbelievably bad shape. Don't immediately discount a deal if it is advertised with available financing, but do expect a fair amount of distress. In my best seller-financing deals, I had to *convince* the seller to carry back financing. These were deals that were distressed but not terribly so.

Once you have analyzed the deal, you'll be ready to make an offer for seller financing. If the seller accepts this offer, you will need to verify the seller has equity in the deal to give you the financing. This is one of the drawbacks to seller financing. If the seller has a mortgage on the property, then they can't finance it to you, and you won't be able to take possession of the title. If the seller has a mortgage, a Master Lease Option (MLO) may be a better way to go.

Important Note: Some investors will do what is called a "wrap" or "subject to" financing. This is where a seller keeps the existing mortgage in place, and the new buyer makes the payments for the old owner. I don't agree with this type of financing at all! The seller is giving you interest they don't have. They are "wrapping" your mortgage around the existing mortgage or allowing you to take over the deal, subject to the existing mortgage.

This can violate a "due on sale" clause that's in the seller's mortgage. This clause states that if the property is sold, the mortgage balance is due at the sale of the property. This means you won't get a title and don't actually have any rights to the property. If you put any money down, you could lose it easily. If the bank finds out there's a new owner operating the property and the mortgage was not paid in full, they have the right to make the full balance of the loan due immediately.

Most advocates of this type of financing will tell you the lender won't care about this type of transaction as long as someone makes the payments. This may or may not be true, but either way, you are taking a large risk. I don't want you to confuse this with seller financing. If a seller has a mortgage, then it needs to be paid off before they give you financing. You want to research the property and find out about the mortgage before you give the seller any money.

PRICE VERSUS TERMS

You should always try to get the best price for any property you are trying to buy (this goes without saying), but most buyers and sellers tend to focus too heavily on price. Sellers also tend to be more sensitive to the overall price they will get for a property and less focused on the terms of financing.

Price makes a big difference when it comes to exit strategies, and you should never pay too much, but the terms of the loan will make or break the operations of the deal while you have it. The terms of the loan include:

1. Term (length of the loan)
2. Interest rate
3. Down payment
4. Amortization schedule

As I've discussed already, you need to solve problems and bring value when seeking CSF. If a seller is going to provide you with financing, then you need to be prepared to give a higher sales price.

HOW TO GIVE ON THE PRICE AND TAKE ON THE TERMS

In many cases, I've given the seller most or all of the asking price when they were willing to carry back the financing. My rule of thumb is, the more distress a deal has, the easier it is to get into. If a seller has a distressed asset, wants a high sales price, and I must get a mortgage and qualify for a loan, then I'm not likely to be interested. If a seller has a distressed asset and they are willing to help me solve their problems, then I'm interested! You shouldn't have to jump through too many hoops to help someone else solve their problems.

In the fall of 2015, I bought one of the best deals I had ever seen. A portfolio of 196 apartments in middle Georgia, consisting of three smaller properties ($26,531 per door). The asset was in fine shape physically but had low occupancy due to the seller's personal neglect.

Due to the low occupancy, I was only able to get a high interest rate, short-term loan from a commercial lender. The monthly payments to the bank were going to kill the deal for me; the property wasn't producing enough cash to cover the note.

As a solution, I got the seller to carry back a second mortgage with an interest rate of 0 percent. This effectively reduced the amount of money I needed to borrow from the lender, and it made the deal work. The seller got the overall price he wanted, but he had to help me on terms to get the deal done. Give on price, take on terms.

If you are paying more for a property, then you need to be overly aggressive with the terms of seller financing. You need this property to cash flow on a monthly and annual basis, regardless of what you pay for it. Keep in mind that seller financing does not have to be 100 percent of the loan. Sometimes a seller can assist with the down payment by taking back a second mortgage. Here are some factors to consider when structuring the loan.

INTEREST-ONLY PAYMENTS

If a deal does not have good cash flow at the beginning, try to negotiate interest-only payments. This allows you to keep more rental income to service the property and to allow for cash flow. You can even offer to make interest and principal payments when the deal begins to make more money.

An interest-only (IO) loan is ideal when the monthly payment is much less than if you were to pay principal *and* interest. The lower monthly payment will allow you to produce more cash flow while maintaining the same amount of rent due. This allows you to spend the cash flow to stabilize the asset.

DEFER ALL INTEREST AND PAYMENTS TO THE END OF THE LOAN

If a property needs major renovations, then defer all or some of the payments to the end of the loan. If the seller wants to start receiving a check at any point during the loan, you may also try to get them to defer payments during the repositioning of the property.

For example, if you decide a property needs X amount of repairs that will take X amount of time to complete, then you'd inform the seller that payments for those months will be added to the purchase price and paid at the end of the loan. This will allow you to complete the necessary repairs while the property is not cash flowing. It's particularly important that you don't over encumber a property with added expenses as you are bringing it back to life. If a seller doesn't see it that way and must be paid even when the deal doesn't make money, then that may not be the right deal for you. Let them handle it on their own.

INTEREST RATE

You should not expect to get the market's most competitive interest rate when you get seller financing. You should try to get the best interest rate you can negotiate, but you also need to offer an interest rate that will be attractive to the seller.

Keep in mind it's not unusual to pay 2–3 percent more in interest than the current lending rates at your local bank. This is not expensive when you consider all the benefits of having the seller finance the deal for you. Whatever interest rate the seller may want, you need to make sure the interest plus principal (debt service) allows you to cash flow the property after you have completed the repairs and leased the units.

Here's another important point: there's a legal minimum required interest rate for private loans. This minimum interest rate is called the Applicable Federal Rate (AFR) and sometimes called the arm's-length rate. This is the minimum interest rate a private lender can give without violating federal law. The law was put into place to prevent people from "gifting" assets to others (usually family) by calling it a loan with a 0 percent (or incredibly low) interest rate. This would effectively allow someone to transfer wealth while avoiding gift or transfer tax. Therefore, the federal government created the AFR.

This concerns you directly if you are getting (or giving) private loans. If you get a loan or seller financing with an interest rate below the AFR, the IRS may consider that a gift, not a loan. The lender may be charged punitive fees and an income tax. This could have terribly negative consequences for you and your lender. Internal Revenue Code (IRC) Section 7872 governs the AFR, and the rate changes periodically. You'll need to consult with an accountant and visit the IRS website for updated minimum rates. This will keep you and your lender in compliance with this tax code and help avoid any unnecessary lender surprises.

DOWN PAYMENT

This is an area where you can get creative. Try to put down as little money as possible but just enough to make the seller comfortable with the deal. If a property needs repairs, then follow this one simple rule: use the down payment to make the repairs.

Decide how much cash it will take to complete the needed renovations. You will make this decision during your analysis and inspection period. Instead of giving the seller the down payment directly, use that money to fund the needed repairs. You don't want to give the seller a cash down payment and then be in need of money to do the repairs.

If the seller doesn't agree with your use of the down payment for the repairs, explain that if you were to default on the loan and they took possession of the property, it would be in better shape than when they gave it to you. You can also offer to put this down payment into a third-party escrow account. This allows the seller to see that the money exists and that you have the cash to do the repairs. You can then draw out the money as the seller approves the work you are doing. This added level of security will help convince some sellers to give you financing.

REPAIRS

Once you obtain the property, you'll likely be responsible for the repairs and cost of operations on the property. This is okay because you'll be using the income the property produces to do these repairs. The difference between the expenses and what the property produces is the cash flow, and you get to keep that!

You'll need to be prepared for any larger repair expenses. These are known as capital expenditures or cap ex. Budget for them by setting aside a capital expense reserve account. Take a portion of income from the property and set it aside to pay for these expenses. I suggest setting up an escrow account outside of your normal operating account for this money. This will keep you from spending your savings on normal operations.

A good rule of thumb is to save about $250–$300 each year for every unit on the property. This will create your cap ex reserve account. It's good to get in the habit of doing this for two reasons. First, it helps protect against the risk of unbudgeted repair items. Second, if you refinance the deal with a bank, it's likely they will make you set this money aside as part of the loan.

INSURANCE

If you're going to be a new owner with seller financing, you'll likely need to get your own insurance policy. Contact local agents to get the best prices. Make sure price is not the only factor you consider when getting insurance. Cheap insurance won't come with much coverage. It's hard to give a rule of thumb for insurance pricing per unit as the information changes so quickly, but in general, it's important to talk with insurance agents when you're analyzing deals.

TAX BENEFITS

As the new owner of record, you will now receive the tax benefits of the property. This is good for you. If the owner wants to retain the tax benefits, then an MLO may be better than seller financing. Consult an accountant to discuss your tax strategies before the closing. I suggest you do this during your due diligence period on the property.

RECORD THE TITLE

This is a tremendously important step in any form of creative financing, especially in seller financing. I strongly suggest you have a real estate attorney create the contracts and documents for any creative financing deal. You'll be able to find seller financing documents and MLO contracts online, but you must have your legal counsel review anything before you submit it to the seller.

Next, have an attorney or title company conduct the closing. They'll be able to do a property title search to make sure the seller can convey a clear title to you. It would be a disaster to give the seller a down payment and take possession of a deal, only to find out they didn't tell their business partner (who also has ownership) what they were doing. An attorney/title company will clear the title. If any existing liens appear, then you will be notified before you close. I assure you, this will be money well spent!

POINTS TO REMEMBER

A seller cannot finance equity they do not have. Seller financing will only work if the seller has no underlying mortgage. If the seller does have a mortgage, you need to have enough down payment money to pay off the original debt. If the loan amount is more than your down payment, you can't offer seller financing. You should move to make an MLO offer.

You'll likely be making offers at or near full asking price if a seller is going to carry back a mortgage. If this is the case, make the terms (interest rate, length of loan time, down payment) highly favorable to you. Negotiate terms that allow for the most amount of cash flow. Use that cash flow to fix up the property.

Always utilize the services of an attorney. Have legal counsel create and/or review all documents before executing them. If a seller does not have an attorney to represent them during this transaction, you should demand they seek legal counsel as a condition of your contract. This is for your own protection. Your seller could make the argument that you took advantage of them somehow with the contract, but if the seller was represented by legal counsel, it makes it harder for them to claim ignorance or to claim you took advantage of them.

ACTION ITEMS

Start the process of building your legal team. Even if you don't have any deals yet, it's a good idea to start looking for an attorney with creative financing experience. This is most applicable to MLOs. Most commercial attorneys are familiar with seller financing but may be less experienced with MLO contracts. Seller financing is typically less complicated than an MLO.

Start this process by networking. Ask local real estate investors who they use. You may be able to find good references at your local real estate investment association (REIA) group meeting. There are also many online groups specific to the multifamily industry. Try networking for referrals there.

When speaking with a prospective attorney, ask about their experience with seller financing mortgages and MLO documents. Notice, I said to ask about their *experience*, not their knowledge. You don't need an attorney who has read about MLO and CSF deals. You need one who has done them.

CHAPTER 6

EQUITY PARTNERS VERSUS DEBT PARTNERS

Although there are many types of investors (partners) in real estate, I will focus on two: *equity partners* and *debt partners*. These two will be the most common in most real estate deals, and both can be used for CSF deals.

An *equity partner* is someone who invests in your deal, and the return on their money is based on the performance of the property. They'll own a percentage of the LLC or legal entity that holds title to the property, or they're on the title themselves.

Here's an example. You purchase a property with traditional financing. The lender requires you to put 20 percent down. You don't have cash for the down payment, so you go to an investor. They join you in the deal by providing the down payment and taking a portion of the equity and cash flow. Their return will be based on the performance of the property.

This type of investment is known as *syndication*, and with it, it's likely you have created a security. There's nothing wrong with this if you do it correctly and you have a Securities and Exchange Commission (SEC) lawyer set it up for you. Attorney fees can be expensive, depending on the size of the deal and type of investors, so this may not work for smaller deals due to the costs.

This is not a lesson on SEC regulations or how to syndicate real estate deals. Just keep in mind that if an investor/partner puts money into your deal and has no control over the production of their return, you are likely creating a security.

A *debt partner* is someone who lends you money to help get a deal done. This person or entity will get a set return on their money. You'll determine the amount before you take possession of their cash.

Just like a bank or any other lender, debt partners set the interest rate, and you make payments to them each month. Assuming you don't default on the loan, the lender or debt partner will get the same monthly payment regardless of the property's performance. The equity partner, on the other hand, will get a return that is largely based on your efforts.

Here's the main difference between equity and debt partners: equity partners don't go away, whereas debt partners do. Once you exit a deal and pay back a lender, the debt partner is done. Once they are paid, the deal is all yours.

An equity partner, on the other hand, owns shares or interest in your company and/or the property they invested in. If you return their capital to them without selling the asset, they still own the equity. Here's an example: You take money from an investor for the down payment and then refinance the property, giving their money back from the proceeds of the refinancing. In this case, they own equity, not debt. If you give them back 100 percent of their invested cash, they will receive an infinite return on their investment until you sell the asset. They don't go away like a lender. Keep this in mind when deciding your exit strategy.

Debt partners want a good return on a safe loan. The interest rate needs to be more attractive than that of other investments in the market. Once you have found someone willing to lend you money on real estate and have set the rate, you're securing the loan with the property itself. This is when you need to make big sales pitches to get people interested in becoming a debt partner with you.

Explain to them they will be lending you money to buy the property (and possibly fix it up) and that the money they lend you will be backed by the property itself. They will have a first-position mortgage on the property. If you were to default, they'd take possession of the property before any other lenders (which is first position). Be prepared to explain how this type of loan works and what a first-position mortgage is.

Some of the best loans come from private lenders. These people may not be professional lenders and may not know how this works. However, the more comfortable you can make them with this process, the more likely they are to do business with you. It's also a good idea to have a business plan for yourself and for the property. Here are some factors to put into the plan for the property:

1. Price (explain why it's a good price)
2. Comparable sales in the area
3. The market and submarket (2–3 miles around the property)
4. The plan for renovations and how that will increase revenue and value
5. Time frame for repairs and to lease the available units
6. Cost of repairs
7. Management
8. Exit strategy and how the lender gets their money back

You can also use this business plan as a marketing piece. It will build others' confidence in you and in your project. It's a way to fully showcase what you are doing and how you will do it.

The last step in this process is to have an attorney create and record your mortgage. I'm in an "attorney state" where real estate attorneys do our closings. You may live in an area where a title company does this. Either way, don't try doing the paperwork yourself. Have the title company or attorney create the mortgage and facilitate the closing.

HOW MUCH DO YOU NEED TO BORROW FROM A DEBT PARTNER?

There are a few formulas that apply to all forms of CSF, not just to debt partners. The amount you need to borrow is an important part of these formulas.

After you have analyzed the deal, you'll know the cost of renovations and the amount of operational "rehab" you'll need to do, such as raising occupancy or increasing collections.

Each of these tasks comes with a price tag, and you need to know exactly what that will be since this is the foundation for your financing offer or loan structure.

If you get seller financing, then you may need to use the down payment money or raise private money to do the repairs. If you are dealing with only a debt partner, then you'll want to raise as much of the total project cost as possible.

During your initial due diligence on a property, you'll get quotes from repair contractors to estimate the amount and cost of any needed repairs (more on this in chapter 10). Use the quotes from the contractors during your analysis to create a loan amount. Show the lender the quotes so they can see how much is needed. Having this number will also help you explain the overall project to your creditors.

When dealing with multifamily properties that need to be renovated, there is one major mistake people often make: they underestimate the time it will take to reach stabilization!

Stabilization occurs when a property has 85 percent occupancy or more with stabilized collections. When doing a multifamily rehab job, you need to know how long it will take to reach stabilization and how much it will cost. To find out, you'll want to consult with local property managers and get a feel for the *absorption rate* in the local area or the number of rent-ready units you can expect to lease in any given month. This is critical information, as multifamily renovation projects rarely cash flow in the beginning stages.

In summary, you need to know the cost of renovations plus the time and cost of stabilization. You may need to have some cash reserves to cover a mortgage payment or the cost of general operation until the property leases up and produces income on its own. Plan carefully!

Here's my general rule for deciding how much money I need for a project:

Purchase Price + Renovation Costs + Refinance Costs ≤75% LTV

Translation: You need to add up all the costs associated with the transaction. This is the price of the asset (purchase price) plus any money to fix up the property (renovation costs) plus money to refinance the deal (refinance costs). This total must be equal to or less than the loan to value (LTV) a lender is willing to give you on this asset. In this case, a refinance is the exit strategy, and it's usually the most expensive. If you plan to sell or assign the property, then calculate for whatever that expense would be. You'll need to be familiar with the lending environment in your market, and I'll cover this formula in more detail in the Exit Strategy section of the book.

I created this formula to give myself a conservative way to calculate the cost of a rehab job. I always calculate refinancing with a traditional lender as the default exit strategy, and you always want to have more than one available exit strategy. If you pay too much or go over your repair budget, this may put a price tag on the property that won't allow you to refinance unless you use your own pocket money to cover the difference. This will limit your exit abilities, and you don't want to be caught in that situation.

HOW LONG DO YOU NEED THE MONEY FOR?

One of the most important tasks in CSF is making sure you set up the agreement correctly. The length of the financing structure is one aspect you want to get right.

If you borrow money from a debt partner or get financing from an owner and the loan time isn't long enough, you can find yourself in a bad situation. Here is my formula for deciding how long to borrow money. This assumes some level of distress and renovation for the property.

Rehab Time + Stabilization Time + Time for Exit = Loan Time

Translation: You want to create a loan with your debt partner that gives you time to buy, fix, and exit the deal. In this formula, *time to exit* is the time it will take to enact whatever exit strategy you are planning. These can include:

1. Refinancing with a traditional lender
2. Sale of the property
3. Assigning the contract (wholesale)
4. Hold and operate

You'll want to decide the parameters for your offer and what financing you'll accept when you do your analysis of the property. You should also know the cost of the repairs and the duration of the project. Finally, you want to know the time it will take to lease up and stabilize the property.

All this information will come from local property managers. Contact management companies in the area to get current information on market data. Also, let them know you need to hire local management as soon as you close your next deal.

I also suggest taking the total amount of time you think the project will take and doubling it for the sake of safety. A seller or lender may not be inclined to agree to a longer time frame, so you have to negotiate the best you can. The longer the financing period, the safer the deal is for you.

Selling and refinancing take the longest time. Before you complete the CSF transaction, you need to consult with the banks or traditional lenders you plan to refinance with. I'll cover this in detail in the Exit Strategy section.

RENOVATIONS WITH DEBT PARTNERS

If you're going to take on a distressed asset that needs physical rehab, debt partners are a great tool, but they do come with some risk. Remember, you owe them money regardless of how your property operates.

Here's the problem: Many people underestimate the total price of renovations. I have done this myself! If you underestimate the cost of repairs, you might not borrow enough money to bring the property up to an operational level. Unrenovated units will not rent and produce income. You might quickly run out of money, and you won't have enough rent-ready units to produce income to pay back the debt partner. This could put you in a foreclosure situation with this private lender. I have been here personally, and it's no fun! I underestimated a large renovation job and had to use my personal credit cards to fund the remainder of the deal.

My first 3 years in real estate were in the single-family space. I had a line of credit with a local bank. I used the money to buy five houses with cash from a single seller, and the houses were junk when I bought them. The seller was about to go into foreclosure when my all-cash offer saved her from it. Each house was going to cost me about $15,000 for carpet, paint, and general repairs. I planned to use the money from the line of credit to fund the purchase of the assets plus the renovations. I'd refinance at a different bank when the work was done and pay back the original line of credit.

This was a great idea until I missed the budget on the renovation costs. I was out of cash on the line of credit and had to finish the project with credit cards. I was able to pay back the credit cards from cash flow and the eventual refinance of the property, but that was not what I wanted to do with my money.

Please learn from my mistake and be incredibly careful when estimating the cost of dealing with a distressed asset. Remember, you're using someone else's money to do the job (even if it's on a credit card).

NETWORKING TO FIND DEBT PARTNERS

You never know when you may be talking to the "millionaire next door." I have raised millions of dollars in private funds from people in my everyday surroundings. To close most of my early deals, I raised over $750,000 from an attorney I knew.

The point is, you never know where the money will come from. So look everywhere. One way to do this is to always talk about real estate. Let everyone in your world know that you are buying properties. Anytime someone asks, "What do you do?" use it as an opportunity to network. No matter what your job is, really, you're a real estate entrepreneur. I don't care if you're a doctor or a rocket scientist. When someone asks you this question, answer, "I'm a real estate entrepreneur, but in my spare time, I'm a [fill in your profession]."

When someone asks me this question, I always use it as an opportunity to strike up a conversation about real estate. I buy apartments, so I might enthusiastically say I'm going to look at a hot apartment investment. I will be excited but vague, and if the person asks for more information, then I'll go into a more in-depth conversation about investing in real estate. I always end the conversation with this remark: "And I'm always looking for partners, if you know anyone who might be interested."

When you first start in the creative and seller financing business, you will hear one common objection from investors: *You haven't done this before, so why should I invest with you?*

You will run into this objection in conversations. You will run into it when you do your first large commercial deal. However, once you close a deal or two, you won't hear it anymore.

If you are new to the business and hear this rejection, don't disagree with the person. Agree with them! Tell them they're right; you haven't done a deal like this before. Then use your education to overcome this objection. Showcase the knowledge you have from this book. Discuss your market and why the deal is such a good deal. Discuss your plans for the property. If you don't have a deal at this point, discuss the real estate market in general and use your knowledge as a résumé.

Your education will carry you to experience. No one starts anything with experience, yet everyone must start somewhere. Just get started.

BACK TO THE 3 PILLARS

Now that we've discussed debt and equity partners, let's overlay this concept with exit strategy and market cycles. If you plan to use equity investors, you need to consider this when analyzing a deal. Do you plan to exit with a refinance? What percentage of the investor's capital do you plan to return from the lender's proceeds? Do you plan to spend any of that money on additional renovations to the asset? What will be the investor's return once you give back some of their initial investment?

When the market is on the rise, you want to use debt partners whenever possible. When the market is rising rapidly, you have more opportunities to refinance or sell. Use short-term debt; it may be expensive when considering the interest rate but will be less expensive on the exit.

When the market starts to decline or go into recession, that's the time to buy and hold long term. Get long-term debt with equity partners who want to be in an investment for 5–7 years. In an up cycle in the economy, everyone wants to invest in real estate, when they should be using cheap debt instead. When the recession hits and everyone should be investing, debt and equity can be scarce.

So in the recession cycle of the economy, one of the best techniques is combining private debt with creative financing. With a few good relationships with private lenders, you can build an entire portfolio.

POINTS TO REMEMBER

Understanding the difference between equity and debt is imperative. Debt goes away when you pay it off, but equity is there for the life of a project. Equity partners don't just go away when you give them their money back. Remember this when analyzing a deal and deciding an exit strategy. Will you bring on a partner or borrow the money? How will you get the seller the down payment or option money for a Master Lease Option deal?

By using CSF offers, you can limit the amount of cash you need to get into deals. Ideally, you will be able to use cash flow from the asset to renovate the buildings themselves. Remember to always limit the amount of investment capital needed to complete any deal. It's not the same as "no money down" but limiting the amount of cash needed.

Investor dollars will cost you equity. To get people to join you in your deals (as investors or partners), it will cost you part of the deal. That's one of the main reasons why CSF deals can be a great way to build wealth. You get to keep more of the equity and overall profits if you can get the deal with a creative offer, limiting the amount of outside cash needed to close.

ACTION ITEMS

In chapter 3, I suggested you begin networking for sellers. Now it's time to begin the same process to find potential partners. I suggest reading some books about networking. There are many good sources of information on this subject.

Don't wait until after you have a deal to start networking. This is one of the biggest mistakes I see people make. It's common to want to approach potential investors or partners with a deal "in hand," but this is a mistake. Once you need cash, it's too late to start looking for it. If you think you're going to meet and establish a meaningful relationship with a potential partner or investor in the amount of time it takes to close a deal, you're in for a harsh lesson.

Start building your base of potential partners and investors now. Start with friends and family. By having conversations with people close to you, you'll build your confidence. Start conversations by explaining why you are interested in real estate investing. Your enthusiasm will help sell your audience on the idea of backing you in a deal. Once you've met with all of your close contacts, start networking in new forums. Find one new meeting per week, and meet three potential new investors a week to get started.

CHAPTER 7

MASTER LEASE OPTIONS

A Master Lease Option (MLO) is a contract between a seller and a buyer that does two basic things. It allows the buyer (you) to control the operations of the asset and the future sale of the property. The MLO consists of two separate documents: the master lease and the option to purchase. The lease allows you to control the asset, whereas the purchase option allows you to control the future sale.

Here's an example of an MLO: Gino agrees to a MLO offer from Susan for his apartment complex. The master lease allows Susan to sublease the apartments to the tenants. Susan is taking control of the property by "renting" the entire property, with the right to sublet the units.

In short, Susan has the ability to manage and control the property. She may hire a management company, or she may choose to manage it herself. The option to purchase (option memorandum) allows Susan to set a price for the property today, with a sale date sometime in the future. She can rent the asset while getting ready to purchase the property.

If an MLO is done correctly, the value of the asset should rise above the option price that was negotiated during the time of the contract (the option period). After it does, you'd exercise your option to purchase. The MLO works for all types of assets, whether a 200-unit apartment complex, a single-family house, or anything in between.

THE PURCHASE OPTION

The purchase option of an MLO contract is the portion that gives you control over the sale of the property and is usually the part that comes with a price tag. An option is exactly what it sounds like. It gives the buyer (you) the "option" to purchase a particular property within a set amount of time for a set price. The buyer usually pays a certain amount of money for the right to hold this option during the option period. This money is called option money and is treated as a deposit.

The option money is given to the seller (or put in escrow) at the time of the MLO contract execution. This money "buys" the rights as stated in the option document. During the option period, you may choose to purchase the property for the set amount stated in the option contract, or you may choose to let the option contract expire and not purchase the deal. If you execute the option to purchase, the option money is applied to the price at closing. If you don't purchase the property within the time frame set by the option, you will lose the option money. This is the risk that accompanies being able to control the sale of the property within a set time.

With an MLO, you have control over the sale in several ways.

The option lets you buy the property for the set amount. It also lets you sell the asset to another buyer if you purchase it first. This may sound complicated, but it's not. Once you have agreed to an option agreement, the price is set in stone and cannot change for the period in which you hold the contract.

If you can find a buyer to pay more than your option price, then you could exercise the option to purchase and sell the property to the next buyer. The difference would be yours. The MLO contract could be sold, too, which we will discuss in the next sections.

EXAMPLE

Imagine you decide to go for an MLO deal. Here are the details:

➤ You get an MLO deal for $1,000,000.
➤ The MLO contract is for 3 years.
➤ In year 2, you find a buyer who will pay $1,500,000.
➤ The price is set at $1,000,000, so you keep the difference.

The catch here is that you need to complete the sale before you can sell the property to the next person. You could use transactional funding. In this case, a lender will come in and lend up to 100 percent of the needed amount but for a notably short time, usually just for two to three days. This allows you to complete the option agreement and then immediately sell to the next buyer.

There are many other options, such as a Transactional Funding. This is a very short-term (24–48 hour) loan at a high interest rate. For now, focus on exercising your option to purchase and close the deal. Then you could immediately sell to the next buyer at the higher price.

As you can see, the option document allows us to not only control the sale but to also benefit from the *profit* at sale. This is a great way to create equity in real estate. Always check with an attorney in the state in which you are doing the deal, because laws regarding closing procedures differ from state to state.

THE MASTER LEASE

This master lease is the other half of the MLO and is a formal rental agreement between you and the owner of the property. The lease allows you to take control of the day-to-day operations of the property, and it will allow you to sublet the units to new renters (or to the ones who are already there). Your duties will be the same as an owner in this position, including management, rent collection, paying the bills, and covering the repairs and expenses of the property. Under the master lease, you could hire new management or become the management yourself.

The value of controlling operations is that it will effectively allow you to renovate the property and improve its operations without the risk of owning the asset. Once it's reached its full potential, you can then exercise the option to purchase, realizing the equity you created between the option price and the new value. The lease portion of the MLO also allows you to control the CASH FLOW.

Note: I often get asked about the difference between a "lease option" and "Master Lease Option." Quite honestly, there is not much of a difference. The term "lease option" is more commonly referred to in the single-family markets, and "Master Lease Option" is referenced when discussing commercial or multifamily deals. If you want to rent a house with the option to purchase later, you get a lease option. This is more commonly known as "rent to own." An MLO allows you to control multiple units at once.

WHY USE A MASTER LEASE OPTION?

An MLO is not the only way to approach buying real estate. It's just one of many ways for you to do deals, and there are many creative techniques for investors to do deals. This technique is just one tool in the toolbox of a skilled real estate entrepreneur. That said, the MLO *is* the best way for a new investor to take control of a property without the hassles of banks, lenders, appraisals, or qualifications.

I've already discussed the requirements for qualifying for traditional financing. Besides the financial aspects of qualifying for a loan, most lenders want you to have experience, too. If you're trying to do a large, multifamily property, you may need multifamily experience to get to qualify for the deal. Experience may not be as much of a factor if you are simply trying to buy a duplex.

As mentioned previously, many people never start to build a portfolio because of lack of funding or the inability to find good deals. The master lease allows you to take control of a great deal with little or no money out of your own pocket. This isn't a "no money down" technique. Those are not responsible. Most deals do require money to get into, but there are ways to get others to join you and help provide that money. Trying to get no-money-down deals can get you overleveraged and potentially damage relationships with agents.

The MLO ultimately allows you to build a portfolio and gain real estate experience without some of the barriers to entry that exist in the commercial real estate market. I'm an advocate of learning how to manage real estate on your own. Learning the management side of the business makes you a strong investor and much more marketable to money partners and lenders. If you are not interested in managing your own assets, then make sure you know how to manage your management companies.

The MLO opens opportunities for many deals that otherwise may not have become a reality. With a bank loan, on the other hand, you must qualify, and the property itself must also qualify. Here are some factors that may limit you from traditional bank loans:

➤ If there are lots of distressed assets on the market, the lenders are less likely to lend.
➤ If a deal has low occupancy or low rent collections, it will not likely qualify for traditional financing. You'll likely need to do a bridge loan (a short term, high interest rate loan that will allow you to stabilize a distressed asset so you can get permanent financing). Lenders' appetites for this type of debt will rise and fall with the strength of the economy.
➤ If values are low or declining, you'll want to find alternative ways to fund renovations. In some market cycles, it doesn't make sense to put a lot of money into a property.

If you look at only a few deals per month, you will find that most properties fit these descriptions.

The MLO is a great way to do rehab projects. It's also good for mitigating some of the risks of doing deals that need work. It's a good vehicle for taking control of something that may not be a good deal but, with work and effort, can become a good deal. Once you turn a property around, you can get a loan and exercise the option you have on the property. You may be able to find a buyer in the meantime and wholesale, or "flip" the deal. Remember, with the master lease, you control the *operations* of the property, and with the option, you control the *sale* of the property.

This technique is also a good way to add units to an already-existing portfolio. Even though you may not technically own the units until you exercise the option, you control the property and the service contracts for that property. This means you may be able to negotiate with the plumber, the painter, the carpenter, and so on, because you now control more units. This is called economy of scale.

In 2012, I added a 108-unit apartment community to my portfolio with an MLO. This increased my economy of scale in that market. Afterward, I was able to negotiate better prices and terms for work on the property because I was able to offer the contactors the opportunity to work on my other assets, too. Economy of scale is an important concept in real estate, especially in multifamily. The more units you have, the easier it is to operate in a market.

Sellers also get a lot of benefits from doing a master lease. Many sellers want to sell because they are burned out from the business. This may surprise you, but not all people are selling property because they need or want the cash. I have done deals where sellers wanted to retire. They didn't need all the cash up front; they just wanted to go and live at the beach but couldn't because of the real estate they had to deal with every day.

Other sellers thought this business was for them and found out they were wrong. They didn't have the education you are getting right now. Still others hired a bad management company and didn't see any cash flow, so they look for a new operational solution.

WHY WOULD A SELLER DO A MASTER LEASE OPTION DEAL?
TIRED OF OPERATING

As I mentioned earlier, this is one of the biggest reasons why a seller would want to give you an MLO deal. You can take advantage of the "burned-out landlord" syndrome and pick up a great deal. If you can solve their headaches, you can get paid.

Also, look for "accidental owners." These are people who have inherited property that they may not know how to operate. Unfortunately, this often occurs after a death in a family. One family member was the operator of the property, and their death put other family members in a tough position. They are now landlords and may not want to be. An MLO offer may be a way for you to help a family or seller in their time of need.

CAPITAL GAINS TAX

If a seller gives you an MLO deal, then they won't have to pay capital gains tax until you close your option (purchase the property). This may solve a major problem for them. Note: If a seller shares in any of the cash flow, they will be taxed for it. They will be liable for taxes on any rent payments you make to them if there is an interest rate involved.

NEEDED REPAIRS

Distressed deals that need some work are a good fit for MLO offers. The seller may not want to put in the time or money to fix up a property, but they're willing to give it to you with a monthly payment that allows you cash flow. You could use that cash flow for repairs to the property.

WHAT EACH PARTY GETS
THE SELLER GETS:

1. Easy sale of the property that does not require a loan
2. Lease payments on the property every month
3. Relief from having to manage the property

YOU GET:

1. A purchase that doesn't involve banks, lenders, or appraisals
2. All cash flow above the lease payment
3. An option to buy at a prefixed price within a set period of time, no matter how much the property value has increased

OVERALL MLO ADVANTAGES:

1. No need for a bank or lender to get the deal done

2. No limit to the terms you can negotiate
3. Quick closing, as quickly as seven days, and low closing costs
4. Seller can generate good interest income each month
5. Buyer can create a good amount of cash flow and equity buildup

THE MORTGAGE

One of the best things about the MLO is that when you take control of a property, you don't have to qualify for a new loan because you aren't actually buying the property. The seller's existing financing will stay in place. You will most likely be the one making the payment, but there will be no change in the existing loan. The mortgage will stay in the name of the current owner, and you can take control of the property the minute the lease contract is executed.

I strongly recommend having the current owner/seller notify the existing lender of the intent to execute the MLO on the property. Some loans have a management clause, which states that the lender has the right to approve all management changes to the property. This could cause a default in the current loan, so I suggest full disclosure.

THE HEADACHES OF THE MANAGEMENT CLAUSE

A friend of mine owned a large apartment complex. He had a management clause in his loan and didn't know it. When he changed management companies without notifying the bank, the bank called the loan due immediately! He had to instantly pay off a several-million-dollar loan. Ouch!

My friend was able to go to the bank and renegotiate; the bank ultimately approved the new management and did not continue with the loan acceleration. But what a headache!

You don't want to be in this situation, so remember that a lender is *your biggest investor* in any deal, and it will serve you well to treat them as such. With a master lease, you are *not* the owner, but *you should act like it*. So make sure the seller has contacted the bank and notified them of the MLO before you execute the deal or give the seller any option money. Take an extra step and ask the bank to give the seller a letter, which states they are aware of the master lease agreement. This protects you and your investment in the deal.

Almost all loans have a "due on sale" clause. This means an owner cannot sell the property without paying off the existing loan. A master lease should not trigger the due-on-sale clause in a mortgage, especially if the lender is getting paid, but you want to be sure that it won't. There's no reason not to notify the bank or lender of this transaction. Remember, FULL DISCLOSURE!

THE INSURANCE

As with the mortgage, the seller's insurance policy will remain in place when you do an MLO deal. Not much needs to be done here, but make sure to get a copy of the seller's insurance plan, make sure the property is covered and that there is adequate insurance.

As the new "operator" of the property, you want enough insurance to cover any losses on the property. You will likely be the one making sure all repairs are done and overseeing any insurance repairs if there is damage, such as a fire or flood. Insurance companies often want 20 percent down when originating a new policy, so the MLO is another way to keep more cash in your pocket, as you won't have to get a new policy but will take over the seller's policy.

KEEPING YOURSELF SAFE IN AN MLO DEAL

Make sure the agreement is recorded and that an attorney helps handle the transaction and closing of the MLO deal. The actual contracts should be recorded with the state. This prevents the seller from selling the property to someone else during your option period.

This contract will be recorded like any other lien or contract for the property. If the seller tries to sell the property to someone else while your MLO is in place, an attorney can research the title and won't allow the sale of the property. By recording the MLO document, you are "clouding" the title to the property, keeping it from being sold out underneath you.

MANAGEMENT

This is the fun part. When I say "management," I don't only mean property management. I mean the totality of controlling the deal. In the real estate business, *control is everything*. This is something I've always heard big-name investors say, but it never sank in until I began to get seller financing and MLO deals under my belt.

Control has nothing to do with ownership. Even if you own a deal, you still may not control it. A master lease is the ideal way to gain control over a property without the liability of ownership. It's the best of both worlds.

That said, when a seller gives you an MLO, they are entrusting you with the operations of that property. This comes with a large amount of responsibility and should not be taken lightly.

With an MLO, you will have control over:

1. Management
2. Paying the bills
3. Contractors
4. Repairs
5. Rent collections
6. General operations

The list goes on and on.

CONTROLLING MANAGEMENT

I am personally in the property management business, so this topic is near and dear to me. Once you have signed the MLO, you are in the management driver's seat. You have the right to hire a management company or become the management.

If you hire management, you have the choice to keep current management in place or find a new company. Assess the current management. Good management creates cash flow. If the current company is doing its job, then keep them; if not, fire them. Here are a few things to consider when looking at current management:

1. Is the property profitable?
2. Is the occupancy good?
3. Is there a lot of deferred maintenance?
4. Is the property over- or understaffed?
5. Do the tenants renew leases, or do they move each year?

These are just a few questions to ask when you consider current management. MLO deals are often offered on distressed properties, and most distressed properties are in the shape they're in because of the management. If you find the current management is doing a good job, then your life just got a lot easier. If not, you must hire new management or take it over yourself.

HIRING NEW MANAGEMENT

Look for a management company that specializes in the size of property you're taking over. If you have an MLO on a single-family house, do not hire the class-A apartment management company. Your account will not be large enough for them to pay attention to it. They will manage your property "when they get around to it." Likewise, do not hire a small firm that focuses on managing houses if you just took over a 200-unit apartment complex. They will not have the proper systems in place, and they will be overwhelmed.

To find the right management company, ask these questions:

1. What other properties does the company manage?
2. What is the average occupancy of these properties?
3. Is maintenance being done properly?
4. How does the landscaping look?
5. Is there a lot of trash on the property?

Remember, you are building a brand and reputation for your-self. An MLO deal has so much more to do with your overall business than just the one deal you have now. People, including the current seller, are watching to see how you perform. If you do a great job and make money for your seller, they will tell others.

You will become known as a person who can solve real estate problems. This reputation will bring you more business. Therefore, it's so important for you to choose your management wisely and watch their operations like a hawk. The real estate world is a small one, and most owners are in communication with other owners and possible future sellers. Act accordingly.

BECOME THE MANAGEMENT

This is your second option. An MLO is a great way to learn the art of property management. You now have control over the deal and management, so why not do some of it yourself? Collecting rents and fixing leaking toilets is not most people's idea of a good time. It's not mine either, but it is a way to learn the most important aspect of the real estate business. When I started in real estate, I had only a few houses and managed them all by myself. I was the repairman, the rent collector, and did everything else to run the properties.

I'm not suggesting you have to follow what I did. What I'm suggesting is that you become functionally familiar with the management side of real estate. If you don't want to do it yourself, you can still be the management company in control of the property, but you can hire employees to do the actual work. This is what I do today. I have hundreds of units and seven employees. I don't personally collect rent or fix toilets anymore. I sit in my office and talk on the phone, making sure everyone else is doing what they are supposed to do.

As my career developed, I realized the power of controlling management. I started managing my properties because I was broke when I started. But by becoming the management company, I've been offered many more MLO and seller-financing deals. My ability to tell a seller that I'm bringing in my team and we'll personally turn their headache property around to make it profitable has been one of the most powerful selling tools.

When a seller gives you an MLO or any kind of financing on a deal, they will want to know what your plan for the property is. What will you do differently than the previous manager? I suggest you have a strong game plan for the things you will do for operations of the property.

Your plan needs to be considerably different from what previous management did. Their lack of management is why the property is in the condition it's in now. By having a strong plan in place, you can convince a seller to give you the MLO deal. After all, the seller knows they will be stuck with the mess if you run the property into the ground.

Here are some areas to consider when presenting a management plan to a seller. Where and how can you improve on these areas?

1. Occupancy
2. Collections

3. Expenses
4. Maintenance
5. Advertising
6. Staffing
7. Contracts with service providers

These are key areas to improve management. You want to present this improvement plan to the seller the same time you ask for the MLO. Keep in mind that it's not good enough to simply point out that the old management was weak in some of these areas. You need to present exactly how you plan to change and improve where the last manager failed.

If you plan to cut costs, you need to be detailed as to how you plan to cut those costs and what effect that will have. If you plan to hire or fire staff, you need to explain why, and how production will be increased with the new staff. If you plan to cut or increase advertising, you need to know what advertising is working and what is not and explain why you're making a change.

The list of ways you can improve a property is endless. As a strategic manager, you will need to develop the skill to assess a property and decide what's gone right and what's gone wrong. Then create your plan to fix it and pitch the seller on the idea of letting you take control and enact these changes. Explain how you will work as the new management and make necessary changes to the property. If you are hiring a management company, share how you plan to personally oversee the company.

Tip: If you are not yet skilled in analyzing the physical needs of a distressed property, here's how you get past that: Let the new management company you plan to hire do the heavy lifting for you. Call around until you find a management company that's willing to come walk the property with you. Ask them to help you create a strategic plan for turning the property around. You'll want to offer the management contract to this company to help get the property under control.

Take this written plan back to the seller and show it to them while submitting your MLO offer. This will make you look professional. They don't need to know the management company helped create the plan. Once you get the MLO in place, hire the company that helped you create the plan, and let them manage the property under your supervision.

CONTRACTS AND CONTRACTORS

Once you take control of a property, you will have control over who does what work and how much you pay for that work. This can make you quite popular or unpopular in the market. The more units you control in each city, the more influence you have over your service providers or contractors.

With more units, you can bring some negotiating weight to the table when you start bargaining for prices. More work will equal better prices. The better prices you can get for jobs like painting, carpet, HVAC, or plumbing, the more you will save in the operations of the property.

Operational savings = more cash flow
More cash flow = better reputation
Better reputation = better résumé
Better résumé = more deals

This is why I was so keen on learning the management side of the business. I learned more money is produced through operational savings than anything else on a property. One of the best ways to save the money is by getting the best prices from people who service the properties.

Once you start to amass units, you'll want to begin creating relationships with contractors in your area. Find people who can do quality work at a reasonable price. The key here is to find contractors who do a quality job, because as you do more and more deals, you'll be able to give them more work and negotiate better prices.

Once you find contractors who do a good job, I suggest you become loyal to them. As your portfolio grows, you'll make more and more money for them, and you'll become a bigger client. The bigger client you are, the faster they'll come running when you need them. This will help you save money and improve operations at your properties.

HOW I MANAGED A MASTER LEASE OPTION: STEP BY STEP

I recently took over a large apartment complex with an MLO. The management in place had been running the property at breakeven for months. On a good month, the owner didn't get any cash flow at all. On a bad month, the owner had to cut a check to the management company to cover the property expenses. OUCH!

After a few years, the owner got tired of losing money on the deal and decided to sell the property. The seller wanted me to buy the complex from him, but it didn't qualify for a loan.

The financial data from the last year of operations was poor, and the property wasn't profitable.

Here's where the fun started. I looked at the historical financial data and went to the seller. I had to make him realize that because the management company he hired ran the property at a loss for the past year, I couldn't get a bank to help finance the deal. Even though it was not a foreclosure, it was a "distressed asset," and banks have enough of those to deal with—they don't want to finance new ones.

This meant I needed to have all cash to buy this deal. I did not have $5,000,000 sitting around in a checking account to purchase the property. So I went back through the financial data and figured out where the old management had gone wrong. I wrote a proposal and made suggestions as to how I planned to fix the problems. Some of the changes I suggested were:

1. Cut one employee. The property was overstaffed, and this would save about $4,000 per month.
2. Cut back on a few ineffective advertising accounts, saving about $1,000 per month.
3. Cancel a few wasteful contracts, such as marketing that wasn't producing any rental leads.
4. I suggested my company take a percentage of the total profits (net cash flow) instead of a management fee, saving another $4,000 per month. If the property was cash flowing, we got paid. If it wasn't, then we didn't.

Next, I met with all my contractors and got bids for the accounts, such as trash collection, landscaping, and pest control. Once I had my written management plan, I submitted it with an MLO offer. I was working with a realtor, so

I asked if this agent and the seller would meet with me in person. I wanted to explain the MLO offer and how, with my management plan, this would benefit both of them. During this meeting, I could also explain why this seller would have a hard time getting a qualified sale on a distressed asset.

Once I was able to meet with the seller and pitch my idea to him, he was on board. What ultimately got me the deal was my relationships with contractors. I had received excellent written bids from my service providers before pitching the MLO offer. I got great bids because I promised the contractors access to a big property that would make them a lot of money, as long as they kept their prices low to help me get the deal.

Note: Unless specifically stated in the master lease portion of your agreement, you likely won't have the right to include the property in any contracts. You are not the owner and will need to have all contracts approved and signed by the actual owner.

As you can see, there is much more to an MLO than just asking for it when you find a deal. You need to have a plan as to how you will help the seller and how they are going to help you. Remember, if you can solve sellers' problems, you will get more MLO deals than you ever thought possible.

HOW I BUILT MY RÉSUMÉ WITH MASTER LEASE OPTION DEALS

Building credibility in the real estate business is one of the most important things you can do. You'll want to start building your real estate résumé as soon as possible, and an MLO deal is an excellent way to start building that résumé.

You'll want to show that you can successfully control real estate assets. If you hire management, it shows you have "asset management" experience. If you become the management yourself, then you can start to build your management résumé as well.

As you gain more property and more experience, your résumé will get more impressive. This will be a good sales tool as you pitch to prospective sellers. It will give you the ability to say, "See what I've done? You should work with me."

I did a 44-unit MLO deal by building my résumé. I convinced a seller to work with me because I brought in my management team, and we turned the property around. I was then able to refinance the deal with a local bank. I'll cover refinancing later in the book.

OPTION MONEY

As mentioned earlier, the option money is the money given to a seller for the right to control the purchase option of an MLO agreement. There's not a set amount that needs to be put down for an option agreement. The amount often comes down to your negotiating skills. Here are some guidelines for negotiating option money:

1. The more motivated the seller, the less you should put down for the contract.
2. The more distress the property has, the less you want to put down.
3. You want to put down enough money to make the deal attractive to the seller but not so much that you create a new financial burden for yourself or the property.

Legally, you will only need to put down whatever amount constitutes legal consideration in your state. Consideration is the dollar amount that must be transferred to make a contract legal. This may be as little as $1 or $10, but this situation is not probable.

You might hear stories of people getting MLO deals for $10 down, but those are outlier deals. I have done a few transactions like this, but they are rare. If you think you can get deals for $10 every time, you will be sorely disappointed when you start reaching out to sellers.

GETTING THE OPTION MONEY BACK

You want a solid plan as to how you will recover your option money. This will also help you decide how much to put down in the first place. The ideal scenario is to be able to recover your option money through the positive cash flow of the deal.

Start with analysis of the asset. How much positive cash flow will the property produce in 1 year? Keep in mind if the asset is distressed, it may not cash flow until you have completed your renovation plans. You want to aim to cash flow back your option money in half the time of the option period.

So if you control an option to purchase a property for 2 years, consider how much cash flow this asset will produce in those 2 years. Put down half that number.

This is a good rule of thumb, but it's not set in stone. You need to be flexible and creative to get real deals done. The main idea is to reduce your overall risk by getting back any cash you have in the deal. In your management/operations plan, you need to incorporate what it will take to stabilize the operations of the property. This will give you an idea of how much cash flow you should produce every month and how long it will take to get the property to cash flow. Use this data to decide how much option money you should be paying.

Remember to consider the time frame the MLO deal will be in place (option period). You won't want a property to take 4 years to repay your option money if you have an MLO for only 3 years. If the contract period for the MLO is 4 years, then you want the property to cash flow your option money back in 2 years. If you get the option money back in half the option period, you will cash flow for the second half of the option period with no financial risk.

Note: If you get to the end of the option period and you don't complete the option and buy the deal, you lose the option money. This is not an issue if you have already cash flowed it all back before the option date. Property operations are never totally predictable, so estimate your time frames and returns conservatively. Leave a large margin of error in your calculations. A good deal should not need to be proven by a calculator; it should be obvious.

HOW TO GET THE OPTION MONEY

The best answer is that you already have it. There are other ways to get it, but they will increase your risk. Here are a few.

BORROW IT

You can find a debt partner to lend you the option money needed for the MLO contract. You must keep in mind that you don't actually have any ownership in the MLO property, so you cannot use the property itself to guarantee the loan. If your partner won't lend you the money on your signature alone, then you'll need to find some other form of collateral that you already own.

The benefit to borrowing the money is that you don't have to have it already, which can lead you to executing the contract faster and possibly doing more MLO deals in a given time frame. The risk to borrowing the money is that you enter into a much more leveraged position. You will need a solid plan to pay back the loan. You can pay it back in the same way you get back the option money—through cash flow.

You will want to pay back the borrowed money in half the time that the MLO deal is in place. Keep in mind you will probably be working for free until the loan is paid back. The asset may not produce enough revenue to pay the loan for the option money and to allow for extra cash flow. Don't let this discourage you. If you get into an MLO deal with absolutely no money coming from your pocket, then it makes sense to work for free. Still, you want to get into a deleveraged position as fast as possible.

You want to pay back the loan ASAP for a few reasons. If someone lent you the money to do the deal, you will want them to remain confident in you, as they might be a source for borrowing future option money.

You also want to build a reputation as someone who can be trusted with private money. If you make your debt partners a good return on their money, they'll be more willing to lend to you again on the next deal.

If you have to borrow money, consider the benefits you are still gaining from doing the deal:

1. You are getting experience in the real estate business.
2. You are getting management experience.
3. You are building a credible résumé.
4. You are controlling an asset that you don't own yet.
5. You are controlling the sale of the property.

Getting paid is nice, but sometimes you must pay your dues. Even though the items I listed above don't come with an immediate cash return, they are worth more than money itself because you can't buy them. Résumé, credibility, experience—these things are investments in yourself that will make you infinitely more money in the long run if you're willing to put in the time and effort in the short term. *So pay back your loans as quickly as you can. Work hard and deleverage.*

HAVE A PARTNER BRING THE CASH

You could also find a partner to join you in the venture for a percentage of the cash flow. This is not a debt partner because they are not lending you the money. In this case, you will want to have this partner join you on the MLO documents. They will be a full partner with you in the deal and will also be named on the agreement contract. They will bring all or some of the cash needed for the option payment and will receive a percentage of the revenues created by the property.

You'll want your partner to be fully involved in creating the management plan for the property, and it will be your responsibility to have this partner fully informed and educated about the MLO process. You'll want to explain the process, risks, and the potential for profit. A partnership that isn't based on full disclosure is a partnership waiting to fail.

Also, don't get greedy with the numbers. Base your projections for the property's cash flow on solid information. Again, you can have a local property management company help create your management strategy for the property. This helps you create an income projection for your partner based on reality.

One of the biggest mistakes I see new investors make is getting overly enthusiastic about projecting a property's profitability to make the investment attractive to financial partners. Remember, you are the one who's running the deal, and you are the one who will have to explain to your partners why the deal isn't operating like the projections you gave them. Be conservative with your projections and always have someone with more experience than you look at your management plan.

WHO PAYS WHAT?

Obviously, a property under an MLO deal still has bills to be paid, such as:

> Mortgage payment
> Insurance payment
> Taxes
> Utility expenses
> Maintenance

Who pays these bills? The likely answer is you, the holder

of a master lease. This is actually a good thing. You'll be the one paying expenses for the property from the income the property produces.

Remember the part about control? You need to make sure you're properly set up before you sign the contract. You *will not* want to give the owner the payments and hope they send the money to the lender or to the tax office. There is a very real chance the seller may not make the payments as promised. If the taxes or the mortgage are not paid, the state or lender will take possession of the property. At that point, your MLO becomes worthless. The state or lender will have the authority to override your agreement with the seller.

To prevent a nonpayment situation beyond your control, set up a third-party escrow account. You'll want to have a title company or an escrow agent set this account up for you. The mortgage payment, taxes, and insurance payments will be placed in the third-party escrow account and paid by this agency. This service is not free, but security and peace of mind outweigh the cost. By involving a third party, there will be no chance of the seller telling you payments were made when, in fact, they were not.

The escrow agent will generate account statements for you and the owner so both parties can see that payments are being made. The seller can see you are doing your job as the operator, and you can see that the taxes, mortgage, and insurance are being paid. This further protects your interest in an MLO deal.

If a seller is not comfortable with you putting the monthly

payments into escrow where everyone involved can see the payments, then watch out! I would not enter an MLO deal and give the seller any option money if they won't allow me to escrow the payments. This is a clean and transparent way to do the transactions, keeping everyone honest. If a seller does not agree, then there's reason to be cautious.

Remember that taxes, insurance, and mortgage are the three main payments to escrow, but they may not be the only ones. Each property will be different and may have other payments you need to escrow as well. You should escrow any payment that could cause the property to default with a loan or could otherwise damage the property financially if it's not paid. Make sure you know what items need to be paid before signing an MLO deal.

POINTS TO REMEMBER

MLOs are a great way to do business, but they are not the only way. *Do not* go around looking for MLO deals. Analyze properties just like you would for any purchase. If the deal fits the MLO model, then you offer it.

The key to an MLO is the analysis. You need a full understanding of what the property needs in terms of physical as well as operational repairs (like leasing, collections, and occupancy). Next, you need to decide how much time it will take to complete the business model. Whatever that time frame is, add 20 percent. This analysis tells you how long the MLO needs to be. Remember to put down as little cash as possible while being conscious of the seller's needs.

Do not do an MLO just because you can. Make sure your

analysis is reasonable when considering the deal, the market cycle, and the area.

ACTION ITEMS

Find three bad deals and make them work with an MLO analysis. This is just for practice. I'm not suggesting you go all the way and make actual offers (but you could).

First, get full financial information on these properties. This includes a profit and loss statement and a rent roll. The easiest way to get this information is to go to the website of a realtor who has some multifamily deals listed. Download the information and do a full analysis. If the analysis shows the price is considerably high for the income of the asset, figure out how to make the deal work by using an MLO model for the analysis.

Do not lower the price to make the numbers work. Solve other issues to get the cash flow you want. If you can't get the numbers to work with the MLO analysis, then you've found a deal that is bad no matter what. It's overpriced. Knowing which deals you shouldn't do is just as important as knowing which ones you should.

CHAPTER 8

FINDING DEALS

"You're an idiot!" All forty-three people in the room went quiet simultaneously. Pin-drop quiet. Everyone was staring at me. I had just closed my first deal on a duplex, quit my career in corporate aviation, and already spent half of the $10,000 in savings that was supposed to last for months... and a guy in the back of the room just stood up and yelled, "YOU'RE AN IDIOT!" This was not how I imagined the start of my real estate career. I took a deep breath, and from across the room I yelled back the only defense I could think of: "WANT TO GO TO LUNCH?"

It was early evening in Macon, Georgia, in July of 2005. Nervously, I walk into my first local real estate investment association (REIA) meeting. This was the very first real estate investor club that I had ever been to. My first deal was going great. I had owned it for about 2 months now.

After a round robin of introductions, all people who were new to the meeting took their seats. The host proceeded to ask if anyone had closed a deal since the last meeting, or if anyone had done their first deal. After a few other people shared their stories, I raised my hand. I stood up and told them about my first purchase: I paid $42,000 for a duplex and it was currently cash flowing quite well. The room busted into applause.

The guy in the back was at least kind enough to let everyone stop clapping before he stood up and yelled out, "YOU'RE AN IDIOT!"

His point in telling me and the rest of the room (loudly) about my idiocy was that I had paid too much for a duplex. He repeatedly said that he and everyone else (not including me) had paid about $20,000 for the other duplexes on that street and most of the surrounding cross streets. Whoops. Yes, I took that guy to lunch.

The two great lessons I learned about finding deals were:

1. If someone says you're an idiot (or any version of that), check your ego and find out why they think so. You can disagree with them later, but first, try to learn something.
2. Place the deal into the context of the surrounding market. Namely, you must always use more than one way to analyze a deal. I only used income to value the deal. I didn't pay attention to what everyone else was paying, and I overpaid. A lot.

In this chapter, I will cover how to identify distress and how to market for deals. The next chapter on deal analysis will teach you how to review the financials and the property to figure out whether or not a deal is for you. These two chapters will help set you up to make an offer.

The first step to finding creative financing deals is to *not* find creative financing deals. Yes, you read that right. The biggest mistake you can make when it comes to CSF deals is thinking this is the only way to get deals financed. You need to look for deals in all the same ways you would look for any deal. If you go around looking for only creative financing deals, you'll miss many opportunities to buy great assets that may be good deals but just aren't fit for a creative offer.

The second most common mistake is asking sellers or realtors for creative financing too early in your relationship with them. Don't call a realtor for the first time and ask if they have deals that offer seller financing. If you ask for creative financing early on, you may send the wrong signal to a realtor or seller. You may be sending the "I have no money" signal. That's not good. You never want to be perceived as broke or financially incapable of purchasing real estate (even if it's true).

Realtors and sellers won't work with you if they don't think you can close; they think you'll waste their time. You need the seller and/or realtor to believe you are more than capable of buying the asset and you are too smart to buy a bad deal. If the asset is distressed in some way, you can help solve their problem, but only if they are willing to help you solve it (creative financing).

If the realtor or seller isn't interested in receiving help with their problems, that's fine by you, because you know plenty of other sellers and realtors who are more than happy to help you solve their problems. That's the attitude you need to display. You are not stupid, and you will not buy a bad deal. You can close but only on good deals, and you are here to solve problems.

There are opportunities to find creative financing deals in any economic cycle and in any market if you know what to look for. Keep in mind that even in the best economy, there are still cities and neighborhoods that may be on a down cycle or have been depressed and are now gentrifying.

There are opportunities to find value-add deals everywhere, but this doesn't mean all value-add deals are good deals. Not all opportunities are good opportunities. Not all distressed assets are created equal. Some are just junk. Your job is to be able to tell the difference between good and bad distress and to create value in that area of the market. You should never do a deal just because you can.

IDENTIFYING DISTRESS

Let's discuss how to identify the difference between a property that has an acceptable level of distress compared to a property that is too far gone. By deciding what level of renovation and distress you are willing to deal with, you can better identify when and where to make offers.

GOOD DISTRESS

1. Bad management
2. Low occupancy
3. Minor repairs (carpet, paint, etc.)
4. Low rents
5. High expenses
6. Area has been depressed but is now in a zone of revitalization

BAD DISTRESS

1. Structural damage
2. Large areas of exterior damage
3. Large amounts of wood rot (interior or exterior)
4. High rent-delinquency rate
5. High tenant turnover
6. Property in a high-crime neighborhood

Start with these lists when you begin looking at listings. There's no need to seek out distressed assets specifically. You will come across plenty of them when you begin looking for deals.

HOW TO SOURCE POTENTIAL ASSETS

Anyone who has experience in real estate will tell you that most of the work in this business consists of finding good deals. Using the right tools will maximize the efficacy of that work. Here are several strategies to increase deal flow.

DIRECT TO OWNER

Contacting owners directly works well with smaller assets and becomes less effective as you move toward larger assets (100+ units). Direct mail campaigns work great for single-family homes and have a decline in response rate (closer to 0 percent) as you move to larger assets.

I have sent thousands of letters and postcards in my career. Here are some tips for direct contact techniques:

1. Mail campaigns

A. Automate these if you can. Get a list of names and addresses and outsource the mailing.

B. Choose a specific market. Don't waste time and money randomly blanketing an area with mailings.

C. Set mail campaigns to run in the background of your business. This should not take up more than 5–10 percent of your time or resources.

2. Calling/contacting owners directly

A. Get a list of contact information for owners of buildings in your area.

B. Call or contact them and simply state you are interested in buying their property.

C. Building rapport with a potential seller is important, but once you have an owner on the phone, get to the point. How much are you willing to pay? That's all the seller will care about.

D. Before you call, look at comparable sales in the market and use an average capitalization rate (cap rate) for similar assets. Know what your numbers are before you reach out to sellers.

E. Be willing and able to give a *reasonable* price on the first call. You don't want to call someone and throw out a low-ball offer. You aren't making a full offer here; you're simply letting the seller know what you're willing to pay for an asset like theirs.

NETWORKING

Good old-fashioned networking can be a great source for creative deals. I highly suggest you get involved in your local real estate clubs and meeting groups if you aren't already. If there aren't any good groups in your area, start one.

Most of these groups hold a "haves and wants" meeting where people can discuss deals they have for sale and what they are looking for. This arena is a great place to find potential sellers who may have deals they're willing to finance for you.

When networking for CSF deals, you must be more strategic than simply waiting for someone to stand in front of the group and offer you CSF. You need to listen for problems that could be opportunities for you. Listen for people complaining about a property they have. Listen for clues that indicate they are "burned out" with an investment property.

They may not be done with the real estate business in general, but they may have a headache property they'd like some help with. This could be an opportunity for you to get started. I suggest listening to people in your everyday life the same way. Listen for people complaining about rental properties they own. Burned-out landlords tend to be vocal about it!

Important Note: Don't start a conversation with an agent or seller by asking for CSF. Again, it's okay if you don't have money, but that's not how to get a new prospective agent or seller to take you seriously. You need to let them know their distressed asset is a problem and that you can provide a solution.

FROM THE OTHER SIDE OF SOURCING

I have personally financed other people on distressed assets I didn't want to deal with anymore. I owned a 4-unit building in a high-crime neighborhood, which I had purchased when I was new to the real estate business. It finally cash flowed, but it required a lot of management attention.

As my portfolio grew beyond hundreds of units including large apartment complexes, it was no longer good use of my time to deal with this asset. I could have my managers deal with it, but that would have kept them from managing more profitable and productive properties. My larger complexes made much more than the small 4-unit building.

The way I solved my own real estate problem was by offering a master lease to a local church. This church used these units for a battered women's shelter. The church was paying my mortgage, covering the monthly expenses, and managing the property. I was no longer creating cash flow from the property, but I still received the tax benefits of owning it and didn't have to waste time and money dealing with it. That church could have been an investor like you. If I had found another investor looking for a break, I would have financed that property to them in the same manner.

To reiterate, there are plenty of sellers who have problems or properties they don't want to deal with. If you find these kinds of deals, you get to collect the cash flow. But it's up to you to find sellers who are willing to help you help them.

BUILD A REPUTATION AS A PROBLEM SOLVER

Building a reputation as a problem solver in your market can bring you more CSF deals than anything else, but this will take some time. You need to close some deals and solve a few problems first. It's not good enough to tell people about what you can do; you have to show them.

Once you've done about three to five deals, you need to make sure you get the credit you deserve. This is when you go back to your networking. Start making more appearances at your real estate clubs. Offer to get up in front of the class and discuss the deals you have done and how you did them. You will instantly be elevated to "expert" status. People will talk about you and how you did those deals.

Word will eventually get around to sellers and agents, and they will start calling. At one point, I had an agent bring me a large commercial apartment complex and suggested I make an offer of a master lease with an option to purchase. He knew my reputation for solving problems with creative financing. As a result, I took control of a $5,000,000 asset with only $25,000, all because I had solved problems for other sellers in my market.

WORKING WITH COMMERCIAL REALTORS (AGENTS)

When looking for apartment complexes with fewer than fifty units, it can be best to go directly to owners through direct mail and phone calls. When you start looking at deals larger than 50 units, you start getting into commercial realtor territory. I'm not saying you can't find deals by using realtors for smaller properties or that you can't go directly to owners of large complexes—some deals can go against the norm.

If you are looking to buy larger multifamily or commercial properties, commercial real estate agents are the best source for deals. Owners of commercial property typically don't put a "For Sale by Owner" sign in front of their 200-unit apartment complex or strip mall and hope a qualified buyer drives by. They call the leading agents and commercial real estate brokerage firms in the area to list their property.

Since realtors are a great source for real estate leads, they're also a great source for creative financing leads. The key here is to build a relationship with realtors in your area so you increase your deal flow. Analyze everything and make creative offers when you can.

By building a relationship with the realtor, they'll contact you before they send the listing out to the public. Some of the best deals I've done came from snatching up a good deal from a realtor before anyone else had a chance to look at it. Realtors are looking to get the best price for their sellers, but they also want to close their deals. These realtors must believe in you since they are putting the sale up against your ability to close. No closing, no commission. Realtors want to work with closers and get paid. It's pretty simple.

Be patient when building relationships with commercial agents. Sometimes you must show the agent that your interests align with the creative offer. Show them you know what you are doing and that you can create problem-solving offers. Ultimately, you will get the leads you want.

An important first step in working with an agent is to not waste their time. If an agent believes you are just "kicking tires" or casually looking at properties, they may not take you seriously. To be taken seriously in this business, you must know what you're looking for and what you're looking at. If you know what you're looking for, it means you know what a good deal is and you have a plan to pay for it. If you know what you're looking at, it means you're informed about the asset.

KNOWING YOUR ASSETS

"What are you looking for?" When first contacting a realtor, you need to be able to answer this question. You have about 30 seconds to provide an answer that will make them take you seriously (no pressure). Your answer needs to be both concise and detailed. If you can't properly communicate what you're looking for, the realtor can't find it for you. More importantly, if you can't communicate what you are trying to buy, it's probably because you don't know. And a good realtor will recognize that immediately.

So what are you looking for?

1. Size (number of units)
2. Asset class
    A. A, B, C, or D
3. Area you want to be in
    A. A, B, C, or D
4. Price
    A. Price per door
    B. Total price range
        i. Example: $1,000,000–$5,000,000
5. Capitalization rate (cap rate)
6. Debt-service coverage ratio (DSCR)
7. Cash on cash (CoC), or the return on investment created by cash flow. We'll discuss more about this in chapter 8.

Here is the same list, read in a conversational tone as if I were calling an agent:

Realtor: "Thank you for calling...What type of assets are you looking to purchase?"

Me: "I am looking for C-plus to B-plus-type apartment complexes in B areas, 100–200 units, and I typically pay about $75,000 to $125,000 per door, with a total project price range from $7 to $12 million. I need to see cap rates between 6 and 7, and a debt-service coverage ratio of 1.25 or better. Cash on cash needs to be around 7 percent."

The data and numbers will differ for your specific buying criteria and the market you are in, but this gives you a framework for that first 30 seconds with a new realtor.

Here are a few types of WRONG ANSWERS for the same call:

Realtor: "Thank you for calling...What type of assets are you looking to purchase?"

Answer: "I'm looking for apartments that cash flow a lot."

Or: "I am looking for a really good multifamily deal."

Or: "Got any deals I can get seller financing on?"

Don't ever use the answers above. Establish the relationship, analyze the sale, and make a CSF offer when applicable. Simple as that.

When looking to establish new realtor relationships in a market, I suggest you visit realtor websites first. See what listings they have before you call them. Study a deal and call them about that deal specifically. If you have to leave a message or send an email for your first attempt at communication, you're more likely to get a response if you contact them about a specific deal. Even if you don't like that particular deal and have no intention of buying it, you will start the relationship.

If you use this technique, make sure to actually read the listing! My realtor friends often tell me that people who call don't read the listing info. Read the listing so you don't ask dumb questions like "What's the price?" or "How many units is it?" when that information was right in front of you. You'll quickly lose credibility with realtors if you don't seem to be informed on the basics.

CREDIBILITY

Now that you've started calling agents, it's time to discuss an especially important subject: credibility. You don't need to close thousands of units to gain credibility with an agent, but they do need to take you seriously. Once you've closed a few deals, you won't have to worry about credibility. Here are the three most effective ways to gain credibility when you are starting out:

1. Know what you are looking for
2. Know your market
3. Understand the asset

We have covered the first item on the list already. For the second item, "know the market," I mean you should have a working understanding of the city and the economy you are trying to buy in. You should understand the areas in the city that are considered A, B, C, and D areas.

You'll need to know which sides of town have the most development. Which areas are economically depressed? You also need to know the capitalization rates (cap rates) for comparable assets in the market. You can find out a lot of this information by calling the local chamber of commerce or the economic development committee for your area. Local management companies can also be a good source of market data.

You should have an idea about the debt availability in your market and in the national market as well. Understanding debt structures is a great way to gain credibility with a realtor. You need to understand which types of loans (Freddie, Fannie, HUD) are available for each type of assets. Not all loans fit all types of assets. Understanding traditional debt structures helps you to identify when creative financing is a viable option.

Finally, you need to understand the asset. If the agent sends you a distressed asset or the seller is personally distressed, then you make the offer for CSF. First, you need to build the relationship so you can view the property and find out where the problems are. If the agent shuts you down early in your conversations, then the likelihood of getting more information on the deal is slim. Without this critical information, you may not be able to craft a winning offer to solve the seller's problems and get you into a great deal.

TIPS FOR WORKING WITH REALTORS
TIP #1
Find out during the initial conversation whether or not the agent sells the asset type you are trying to buy. I can't count how many times I've called an agent who had an apartment listing but wasn't a full-time commercial agent. Sometimes a single-family agent gets lucky and has a larger apartment

complex listing, and it's fine to work with them if you are interested in a specific property. But if you aren't, don't waste too much time building a relationship with them. They won't have access to the larger sellers in your area.

When I'm on a call with a new realtor contact, I politely ask, "Are you a commercial agent?" You should do the same. If you want to buy something specific such as self-storage or retail space, I suggest looking for a commercial agent who specializes in those property types.

TIP #2

When dealing with a realtor on a property and you want to make a CSF financing offer, get permission from the agent! An agent must legally submit your offer, but they don't have any obligation to *recommend* the offer to the seller. In fact, they can recommend that the seller NOT take the offer.

The remedy for this is to start your CSF sales pitch with the agent first. Explain why this offer will solve everyone's problems, why you are the person for the job, and how the realtor will get paid. You'll likely need to explain how the creative offer will work. If you're offering a master lease, the agent may not know how that works. Spend some time explaining and educating this agent so they can do the same with the seller (whom you may never get a chance to talk to directly). Submit the offer once you have the agent on board.

TIP #3

A good negotiation begins by allowing both sides to take part in creating the agreement, and it's no different when working with an agent. Once you have explained why this offer is a good one, you'll want to get the agent involved in creating the offer.

Ask them for their guidance. Ask them what the seller really wants, and explain that the two of you will create an offer that will help everyone out. If you can get the agent involved in creating the offer, they'll be much more likely to recommend the offer to the seller.

TIP #4

The main objection you'll get from a realtor about a CSF offer is related to payment; they may not see or understand how they will get paid. Keep in mind that the realtor's main concern is their commission on the sale. A listing agreement between an agent and a seller says the agent is due a percentage of the sales price. But what if there's no real "sale" and it's Master Lease Option (MLO) or seller financing instead? What then? I'll give you some tips, but the answer is, you'd better get creative!

One thing you can do is share the cash flow with the agent. It doesn't have to be a lot; share just enough to get them interested. If you are doing an MLO or seller financing, you can also write the agent into the contract. You can state in the contract that the agent is due X amount of money or percent of the cash flow each month and that they'll be due the full commission when you take title and pay off the seller. With an MLO, that would be at the time you exercise your option to purchase. With seller financing, it would be when you execute your exit strategy. Explaining these details will help the agent feel more comfortable about helping you make the CSF offer.

TIP #5

You also need to consider when and how to contact realty agents. I suggest limiting your email contact with them in the beginning. Never make your first contact with an agent through email. It's too impersonal, and they can easily ignore you. Email is a quick and easy way to reach out to people, but it should only be used once the relationship is established. In the beginning, call the agent on the phone. If you don't get an answer, leave a message and call back in a day or so if you don't get a response.

You'll want to get this agent's attention quickly and definitively by getting them on the phone. An email doesn't allow you to do that. And never send a five-page email detailing what you want to say. No one will read it. Instead, you want to showcase your knowledge about the market and real estate quickly over the phone. Once you have established a line of communication and the agent knows who you are, then it's perfectly fine to move to email as a form of communication.

When I contact agents, I've found that the best time to call is Tuesday through Thursday from 9:00 a.m. to 5:00 p.m. On Mondays, people are catching up from the weekend and any work left over from the last week. On Fridays, they are mostly thinking about the weekend. Tuesday through Thursday is the best time to catch them in their office and find them in the best frame of mind.

Not all agents will be a good fit for you. If you call someone and they are rude or short with you, they may not be the best person to work with. If they don't respond to your requests for information, or they want to see that you have millions of dollars in a checking account before they work with you, move on! There are plenty of good agents who are hungry for business and will be more willing to work with you. Don't let one bad conversation frustrate you. Just move on.

TIP #6

Be careful of an "exclusivity agreement." Some agents will try to get you to sign an exclusivity agreement that locks them into being your representative whether they find a deal for you or not. Do not sign this! This is a totally one-sided agreement. This will allow them to take commission from any deal you find in the area, even if they aren't involved in it. This could also cause other realtors to not take your offers seriously because they know they must give half of their commission to someone who did nothing to earn it.

However, it's okay to sign this agreement when it is specific to a deal the agent brought you. You shouldn't attempt to cut an agent out of their commission if they brought you a deal, but the agreement ends there. If an agent tries to get you to sign an exclusivity agreement, then they're trying to lock you down with no risk on their part. If an agent tells me (and some have) that they will only show me properties if I sign this type of agreement, I tell them I'll find someone else to find properties for me.

If they are good agents, they should be confident in their ability to find you good deals without locking you down. If they aren't, then they are likely wasting your time anyway. If an agent asks you to sign this agreement and you want to have a little fun with them, say this: "I will sign your exclusivity agreement if you will sign mine. I'll be comfortable with you being my only agent in this market if I'm the only investor you'll represent in this market." Funny, no agents have taken me up on this yet!

TIP #7

Again, realtors are most concerned with their commissions. Therefore, they may be especially concerned about an MLO. An MLO is not a sale, and the agent may be thinking if they present your MLO offer and the owner accepts it, they will lose the listing and not be paid for their time.

To prevent this from happening, assure the agent they will be paid if the MLO deal is accepted. After all, this agent brought you the deal and should be compensated. Make them happy, and they will be a continuous source of good deals. Get cheap and it will cost you in the long run. Remember, the seller is not getting a check for the sale of the property, so they will be less inclined to cut a check for the agent at closing.

There are many ways to compensate an agent who has worked hard to bring you a deal. Here are some suggestions that have worked for me in the past:

➤ Allow the agent to take a percentage of your equity in the deal. You might offer to make them a partner on the MLO.
➤ Share the cash flow by giving a percentage of your profits to the agent. This will create some positive cash flow in their life.
➤ Have the agent take an IOU for the commissions. Put it into the MLO that they're due the full commission when you exercise your purchase option.
➤ Trade cash flow or equity in some other property you already own.

➤ Get the owner to give some of the option money to the realtor.

In one of the largest MLO deals I ever did (108 units in 2012), the agent accepted a combination of several of these. He got a $500 per month payment regardless of cash flow. My MLO documents stated he would be owed the full commission when I executed the purchase option and closed on the property. The owner also agreed to share some of the option money he received from me at the execution of the MLO contract with the realtor. And I put up $25,000 as option money when I signed the MLO contract.

Unless this agent represents you personally, all agents represent the seller by default. Their fiduciary responsibility is to the seller, so you need them on your side when doing an MLO deal. The agent can make or break your offer, so spend some time making sure they understand and are comfortable with this process. Allow them to take some "ownership" in the agreement, and they'll be more likely to recommend it to the seller.

POINTS TO REMEMBER

Finding deals is the hardest part of the real estate business. If finding deals were easy, you wouldn't be reading this book. Be prepared to go through a lot of bad deals before you get a good one.

Education is the best path to credibility. Don't be overly concerned if you are new or inexperienced in the multifamily business. Everyone is inexperienced...until they are not.

When looking for deals, be prepared to admit your inexperience, but be able to showcase your knowledge.

ACTION ITEMS

Consistent deal flow is the key. If you aren't meeting your weekly goals for deal flow (3 per week at minimum), then you need to find more sources of deal flow, or you need to add more territory to your market area.

Create as many different sources of deal flow as you can. Go directly to owners when you can, and expect to work with commercial realtors on larger assets.

Analyze three deals per week, and add one new source of deal flow every 2 weeks.

CHAPTER 9

DEAL ANALYSIS

Deal analysis is the single most important aspect of the real estate business. In this chapter, you'll learn how to decide if a deal is right for you, and if it's a good fit for CSF.

I break down deal analysis into two categories: multifamily deals and single-family/small multi-unit deals. Analyzing a large apartment complex is quite different from analyzing a single-family home or small multi (2–4 units).

MULTIFAMILY DEALS

When analyzing a potential asset, you should always assume the deal is a good one and that you will be buying it by getting a loan and putting down at least 20 percent. Why? Because that's what most sellers and agents expect us to do.

Once you've analyzed the deal, you will determine an exit strategy and a creative offer that solves the seller's issues if there are any. If there's no distress on the seller's part, you probably shouldn't make a creative offer. If you don't have the ability to purchase the deal through traditional means, just pass on it and keep looking.

So why analyze distressed assets if you think they won't qualify for a traditional loan and you may not be able to do a CSF? Two reasons:

1. You need to fully understand the deal and if it is distressed and why.
2. It may not be a distressed asset. If it isn't, then it may qualify for a traditional loan.

An analysis of a property, whether it's a duplex or a 200-unit apartment complex, has two major components:

1. Financial analysis
2. Physical inspection

Start with the financial analysis first (it's free). When analyzing a deal, there are three reports you need to obtain from the agent or seller. The first is the month-to-month profit and loss statement, and the second is a year-end profit and loss report.

The month-to-month profit and loss statement is just that: a report showing the income, expenses, and cash flow in a month-to-month format. This is often called a T12 or "trailing 12." This report shows you what the property has done over the last 12 months, regardless of where you are in the year. For example, a normal fiscal year runs from January to December, and a T12 will go back 12 months regardless of the current month. With a T12, you can spot trends, such as increases in expenses or decreases in occupancy. This financial statement will tell you the most about a property and its value.

The year-end profit and loss report, or P&L, is a summary of the last year's operations. Unlike the T12, it ends with the previous calendar year and shows the income and expense totals for the year.

The third report you want to see is the rent roll. This shows all current tenants, the amount of rent they are paying, and occupancy of the property.

There are a few key things to look for in these reports to understand how the data translates into a creative offer.

TRAILING 12 EXAMPLE

	January	February	March	April	May
INCOME					
Market Rent	62,665.00	65,065.00	64,042.00	64,746.00	67,142.00
Gain/Loss to Lease	-579.00	-2,742.00	-2,116.00	-1,813.00	-4,159.00
GROSS POTENTIAL RENT	62,086.00	62,323.00	61,926.00	62,933.00	62,983.00
Concessions	-559.50	-100.00	-55.87	-637.47	0.00
Vacancy	-4,002.07	-4,301.92	-3,454.91	-2,215.80	-1,797.83
Write-Offs	-4,143.24	-1,845.09	-2,175.20	-800.64	-5,959.00
TOTAL RENTAL INCOME	**53,381.19**	**56,075.99**	**56,240.02**	**59,279.09**	**55,226.17**
OTHER INCOME					
Late Fees	1,900.00	1,900.00	2,100.00	1,850.00	2,500.00
Application Fee	625.00	750.00	275.00	200.00	325.00
Water Reimbursement	4,124.83	4,096.22	4,122.73	4,276.49	4,312.26
TOTAL OTHER RENTAL INCOME	6,649.83	6,746.22	6,497.73	6,326.49	7,137.26
TOTAL INCOME	**60,031.02**	**62,822.21**	**62,737.75**	**65,605.58**	**62,363.43**
OPERATING EXPENSES PAYROLL					
Management Salaries	3,622.84	3,754.88	2,744.96	2,772.25	3,878.72
Maintenance Salaries	1,939.08	2,055.88	1,728.00	3,610.82	2,613.23
Payroll Taxes	558.94	370.97	526.88	711.62	691.05
TOTAL PAYROLL	**6,120.86**	**6,181.73**	**4,999.84**	**7,094.69**	**7,183.00**
TOTAL MANAGEMENT FEES	**1,856.61**	**2,015.41**	**1,908.92**	**2,125.05**	**1,861.42**
UTILITIES					
Electric - Vacant Units	1,028.53	723.21	222.87	136.60	148.36
Gas - Common Area	63.86	-29.51	56.82	143.94	146.62
Water	2,598.94	2,783.25	4,195.54	3,849.59	8,131.91
TOTAL UTILITIES	**3,691.33**	**3,476.95**	**4,475.23**	**4,130.13**	**8,426.89**
TAXES & INSURANCE					
Real Estate Taxes	2,768.00	2,768.00	2,098.71	2,098.71	2,712.00
Property Insurance	1,458.68	1,458.68	1,458.68	1,458.68	1,458.68
TOTAL TAXES & INSURANCE	**4,226.68**	**4,226.68**	**3,557.39**	**3,557.39**	**4,170.68**
REPAIRS & MAINTENANCE					
Appliance Repairs	0.00	0.00	0.00	104.24	0.00
Electrical Repairs	0.00	0.00	0.00	0.00	145.00
HVAC Repairs	0.00	0.00	0.00	0.00	-146.48
Maintenance Supplies	347.04	253.03	437.63	942.36	106.66
Roof Repairs	0.00	0.00	0.00	0.00	0.00
Unit Interior Repair	35.00	500.00	2,360.00	1,040.60	-1,060.00
TOTAL REPAIRS & MAINTENANCE	**382.04**	**753.03**	**2,797.63**	**2,087.20**	**-954.82**
TOTAL OPERATING EXPENSES	**16,277.52**	**16,653.80**	**17,739.01**	**18,994.46**	**20,687.17**
NET OPERATING INCOME	**43,753.50**	**46,168.41**	**44,998.74**	**46,611.12**	**41,676.26**

June	July	August	September	October	November	December	Total
67,184.00	69,534.00	76,584.00	76,584.00	76,584.00	76,584.00	71,884.00	838,598.00
-3,738.00	-5,729.00	-11,987.00	-12,238.00	-11,532.00	-10,622.00	-5,167.00	-72,422.00
63,446.00	63,805.00	64,597.00	64,346.00	65,052.00	65,962.00	66,717.00	766,176.00
-150.00	-624.00	0.00	-87.74	-357.00	-896.01	-1,846.74	-5,314.33
-5,038.82	-693.13	-1,084.86	-1,544.03	-2,226.40	-2,952.97	-4,452.39	-33,765.13
3,771.53	-1,653.38	-1,992.34	-138.06	-2,779.90	-3,452.84	-835.63	-22,003.79
62,028.71	**60,834.49**	**61,519.80**	**62,576.17**	**59,688.70**	**58,660.18**	**59,582.24**	**705,092.75**
3,100.00	850.00	1,700.00	1,811.00	2,052.00	1,933.00	2,430.00	24,126.00
450.00	450.00	0.00	50.00	300.00	675.00	400.00	4,500.00
4,094.19	4,382.61	4,408.72	4,357.42	4,303.83	4,229.68	4,188.07	50,897.05
7,644.19	5,682.61	6,108.72	6,218.42	6,655.83	6,837.68	7,018.07	79,523.05
69,672.90	**66,517.10**	**67,628.52**	**68,794.59**	**66,344.53**	**65,497.86**	**66,600.31**	**784,615.80**
3,677.99	3,612.34	3,662.80	3,500.89	3,649.47	2,563.82	3,516.70	40,957.66
772.80	769.58	851.83	3,302.32	1,384.28	1,371.39	2,267.37	22,666.58
888.03	440.46	514.31	828.92	427.34	342.81	1,049.92	7,351.25
5,338.82	**4,822.38**	**5,028.94**	**7,632.13**	**5,461.09**	**4,278.02**	**6,833.99**	**70,975.49**
2,131.77	**2,136.43**	**2,102.98**	**2,157.81**	**1,971.37**	**2,009.40**	**2,050.57**	**24,327.74**
94.79	124.20	70.75	83.43	158.68	329.79	150.18	3,271.39
166.95	159.68	125.21	121.26	123.80	116.68	118.91	1,314.22
7,285.87	7,946.33	8,318.11	8,049.43	8,894.85	9,585.62	10,039.26	81,678.70
7,547.61	**8,230.21**	**8,514.07**	**8,254.12**	**9,177.33**	**10,032.09**	**10,308.35**	**86,264.31**
2,712.00	2,712.00	2,712.00	2,712.00	2,712.00	2,712.00	2,712.00	31,429.42
1,458.68	1,458.68	1,458.68	1,609.31	1,309.50	1,309.52	1,309.52	17,207.29
4,170.68	**4,170.68**	**4,170.68**	**4,321.31**	**4,021.50**	**4,021.52**	**4,021.52**	**48,636.71**
196.42	-11.88	0.00	0.00	0.00	0.00	0.00	288.78
0.00	0.00	0.00	0.00	0.00	0.00	0.00	145.00
102.88	-102.88	0.00	0.00	0.00	0.00	0.00	-146.48
557.08	521.26	772.16	646.68	852.59	411.09	419.23	6,266.81
0.00	975.00	0.00	0.00	0.00	0.00	0.00	975.00
0.00	0.00	0.00	0.00	0.00	0.00	0.00	2,875.60
856.38	**1,381.50**	**772.16**	**646.68**	**852.59**	**411.09**	**419.23**	**10,404.71**
20,045.26	**20,741.20**	**20,588.83**	**23,012.05**	**21,483.88**	**20,752.12**	**23,633.66**	**240,608.96**
49,627.64	**45,775.90**	**47,039.69**	**45,782.54**	**44,860.65**	**44,745.74**	**42,966.65**	**544,006.84**

This is an example of what the financial statements should look like for a larger multifamily property. However, not all properties are large, and not all owners keep accurate financial records. When analyzing deals, you will encounter all types of financial reporting, ranging from the example shown here to a shoe box full of receipts, accompanied by a ledger on the back of a napkin.

The less data you get from a seller or a Realtor, the more you will have to estimate on your own, and you should always reflect that in the price. P&L statements are generally set up in the same format. It's also the basic formula for analyzing a deal as follows:

Income – Expenses = NOI (Net Operating Income)

The first portion of the T12 is the income section. It shows rents, vacancies, and other incomes for the property. The total income for a property is known as the effective income. From that, you subtract the operating expenses (not including the loan payment). This gives you the NOI for the property. Then you need to calculate the debt service (mortgage payment).

As suggested, start your analysis as if you were buying this property with traditional financing. Seventy-five percent loan to value (LTV) is a traditionally safe number when considering a down payment for conventional financing. You can calculate the mortgage payment with a simple mortgage calculator. Consider the price, the LTV, the interest rate, and the amortization for the loan. Once you have calculated the annual debt service, you can move to the next level of analysis.

Income – Expenses = NOI
NOI – Debt Service = CASH FLOW!

Will this deal cash flow if you buy it at the asking price? If not, then you need to lower the price to where it cash flows enough to be a good deal. If it's not a price the seller will accept, then you move to a creative offer. But before you make an offer (creative or otherwise), you need to fully understand why the deal is not cash flowing now. Therefore, you must get the T12.

The detail of this financial report will allow you to start the "financial forensics" that lead to your decision of whether or not to make a creative offer and/or what type of creative offer to make. If an agent or seller gives you only a summary of the financial data (profit and loss), then you won't have the detailed information allowing you to see what is going on with the deal. In order to create value through problem solving, you have to see the financials.

In the financial data, look for trends and info such as:

1. Income
   A. Is it declining or increasing?
   B. Is the economic occupancy rising for falling?
   C. Is "bad income" rising? This is money made from late fees, evictions, move-out fees, and returned-check fees.
   D. The last 90 days on a T12 (T3) are the most important. This shows the most recent trends on the property.
2. Expenses
   A. Are total expenses on the rise or decline?
   B. Which expenses are too high?

C. Can you lower the expenses in any way?

D. Are maintenance costs rising or too high?

E. Is the staff overpaid, or is the property overstaffed?

Each deal is different. You may have some or all of these problems, which are opportunities for you to create value. No matter what, you need to ask why the property isn't profitable, and see if you can correct the issues. If the answer is "Yes, I can correct the problems and create value," then craft your offer so the seller will give you a chance to fix the problems.

Note: Just because a creative offer will be accepted doesn't mean you should make the offer. Not all problems are solvable. If a property has issues that are too expensive or expansive (e.g., structural deficiencies in buildings or being in an area with an extremely high crime rate), you need to pass. These are not problems that creative financing can usually solve.

LOOK FOR PROBLEMS YOU CAN SOLVE

Income is the first place to start. If the total income on a property is declining or low, then you have several problems: physical occupancy is low, economic occupancy is low, or both are low.

Physical occupancy refers to the number of people living in the units. How many are rented?

Economic occupancy is the number of "paying" units. A person can live in a unit and not pay the rent. This unit is physically occupied but economically vacant. It's nice to have occupancy, but at the end of the day, you need tenants to pay the rent.

Sometimes you can create value in the income category by identifying the market rent in the area. Is your rent below the market rent? If so, then you may be able to create value by raising the rent. This is known as *loss to lease*. Loss to lease is the difference between market rent and effective rent, or what you are actually collecting.

Next, move to expenses. Roughly, there are two types of expenses: controllable and noncontrollable. I consider existing mortgage payment, taxes, and insurance to be fixed or noncontrollable costs in CSF.

Examples of controllable costs are repair costs, payroll, and other operating expenses. Here is a list to start with when you are looking at cost mitigation as a value play:

1. Repairs and maintenance cost
2. Payroll expense
3. Unit "make ready" expenses
4. Landscaping
5. Trash removal
6. Office expenses (phone, fax, etc.)
7. Pool service

These are just some areas to examine, and they will be different with each deal. The idea is to find areas where you can create value by cutting the expense. You can produce more cash flow through better operations.

1. REPAIRS AND MAINTENANCE COSTS

Try to bring these expenses down by shopping for better/cheaper contractors. Start by getting bids from local contractors. To get the best price, develop a relationship with these local service providers. I like to find contractors who will give me a discount in exchange for my loyalty. I guarantee them all the work on the property (economy of scale) if they give me good service at a lower price.

Having a local team of loyal contractors will help you get CSF offers accepted. By showing a seller you have a team to get the work done, your offer will seem more credible, and more of them will be accepted.

2. PAYROLL

My rule of thumb for employees on multifamily properties is to have two employees per 100 units. This is divided between office and maintenance staff. Using this example of a 100-unit apartment complex, it should be staffed with what I call one in and one out. You need one employee in the office and one out on the property for each 100 units. The first 100 most likely require a property manager and a maintenance supervisor.

A 200-unit complex should have one property manager and an assistant manager. You'll also likely need a maintenance manager and maintenance assistant.

Most management companies tend to overstaff their properties. I've added thousands of dollars back into the cash flow of complexes by properly staffing them. Some management companies also upcharge for employee costs. For example, if an employee makes $20 an hour, they may charge the owner $25 an hour. You need to know this information so you can cut expenses here.

3. TURN COSTS

This is the expense for making a unit ready for renting again after a tenant moves out. This cost will be decided by your contractors. You want to pay attention to the total amount spent each year on turn costs. This information will be in the financial data. If you see high turn costs (not to be confused with regular repairs), then this means one of two things. Either management is paying their contractors too much, or the tenant base is unstable altogether.

If the managers are paying too much to turn a unit, then there may be opportunity to streamline the expenses. That's good! If the turn costs are high and they aren't paying too much for each turn, then they are turning units too often. This means the tenants in the area/property move in and out on a regular basis. Tenant turnover is typically the highest expense on a property.

The longer a tenant lives in a unit, the more money you make. In most apartment markets, the average tenancy is 2 years. This means that on average you will turn over about 50 percent of your apartments each year. 40–50 percent is normal. If you find that tenants move out (on average) less than every 2 years, you may have an economically challenged property with tenants who move too often for you to ever make any real money. Avoid deals with an unstable tenant base. It will be a management nightmare, and you won't have the cash flow you are expecting.

You'll need to do a little bit of legwork to find out which situation you're in. Start with the rent roll. Do you see a large portion of leases that have begun over the last 90 days? This means a large percentage of the tenants have not been living there for long and may not stay. Ask management directly how often units turn over. Ask how much they spend on average to get each unit ready. Specifically, ask them how much their contractors charge to paint a unit or what they charge for "make ready" repairs. You can then compare this to the estimates you received from your contractors and find out if there is an opportunity for savings.

Renovation Tip: In my experience, you can be overcharged the most when it comes to painting. Most painters are accustomed to painting houses, and I have found that only about one in ten painters specialize in painting apartments. So they give you a quote as if your apartment were a three-bedroom house. Find a painter who specializes in painting apartments. If they paint them on a regular basis, they should be able to give you a rough estimate over the phone.

4. CONTRACT SERVICES

Contract services are services provided to the property on a regular or scheduled basis. This is slightly different from the general contractor repairs mentioned above. Contract services include trash removal, landscaping, pest control, and so on. You will likely be working with a company and not an individual contractor for these. These services will likely be on a contract that may or may not survive the sale of the property. Look to see when these contracts are set to renew and begin your negotiations for new prices early on.

5. OFFICE EXPENSES

This is an area where you can save a ton of money and put

cash back on the books. If an office rents their equipment, then you should compare the cost of buying the equipment versus leasing it. I found one office that paid over $100 a month to rent the copier/fax machine. I priced comparable equipment at the local computer store and found I could buy similar equipment for about $1,000. In less than a year, we were saving money and owned the equipment!

Marketing costs can fall under this category as well. Make sure the property is utilizing all the free advertising it can before spending money on marketing. Make full use of the internet and social media before doing paid advertising. Do some research to see what types of advertising have been effective. Not all marketing reaches all tenant bases. If you have an older C-class apartment complex, you may get more traffic from free postings online than from high-level apartment leasing websites, which can be expensive.

6. POOL SERVICE

Once, I took over a property and found out the maintenance manager didn't really know anything about the chemicals that went into a pool. The old management never bothered to make sure he was trained properly. Each month, he guessed at the amount of chemicals to put in.

There are pool stores in almost every city. If you bring them a sample of your pool water, they will test it and tell you how to chemically service your pool for free. The regional manager took this maintenance supervisor to a pool store and got him educated on proper use of the chemicals. It turns out our supervisor had been putting almost twice the amount of chemicals in the pool than what was needed. In the end, we saved money during the summer months while creating a safer pool for our tenants.

7. RENT ROLL

You can get a general idea of physical and economic occupancy from the T12, but you verify the data with the rent roll. Look at the total physical occupancy. Again, this tells you how many people are living there and how many units are rented, but it gives no indication to the economic occupancy. You may need to look a little closer to obtain this information. Start with the "balance" column. Not all rent rolls call it "balance," but what you are looking for is the amount of rent each tenant owes (tenant balance). Look at the scheduled rent for that unit and then find out the balance owed.

What you are doing is looking to see if the tenants are paying their rent. Every dollar you see in the tenant balance column is a dollar owed in back rent. In my experience, once a tenant gets more than 30–45 days behind, they don't catch up. They either skip out or you evict them.

Recently, a student of mine asked me to help him analyze a deal. His projections and numbers looked rather good until I got to the rent roll. There, I noticed the average rent for each unit was about $500 per month. I looked at the balance column, and I noticed almost all of the tenants had a balance of $1,000–$2,000. In other words, most of the tenants owed several months' worth of rent.

As the new owner, my student would need to forgive most of this back rent, or he would have a morbidly large eviction rate. Even though the property had high *physical* occupancy, it had terrible *economic* occupancy. This is a management nightmare for the period in which you want to turn this property around. At the same time, it could be a negotiating point for CSF if you believe you can tackle the tenant turnover. But remember, new vacancies create an immediate expense as you make those units ready for the next tenant.

SINGLE FAMILY AND SMALL MULTIFAMILY

Analyzing houses and smaller multifamily deals (2–10 units) is different from commercial multifamily deals, but the fundamentals are the same.

Income – Expenses = NOI
NOI – Debt Service = Cash Flow

In houses and small multi-units, you again want to look at the income and expenses. How much is the rent? Subtract the expenses and mortgage, and you have the cash flow. A rule of thumb for houses up to ten units is to estimate about 10–15 percent of the revenue in maintenance costs, depending on the age of the property. The older the property, the higher the maintenance costs will be.

Here are the three other things you need to know about single- and multifamily deals:

1. Mortgage payment
2. Annual taxes
3. Insurance costs

Add these three items plus the maintenance, and you have your total expenses. Subtract your debt service, and any income left over is cash flow. You should try to get $150–$300 in cash flow from a house and $100–$150 from each unit of a multifamily property.

Tip: If a property is newer, it usually appreciates faster than an older house. For this reason, you should collect more in cash flow from an older property. If you stand to make a significant profit at resale, then it's acceptable to have less cash flow. Older properties don't appreciate as much, so make sure to get the cash flow!

MASTER LEASE OPTION DEAL ANALYSIS

Remember, a Master Lease Option (MLO) alone doesn't turn a bad deal into a good one. A bad deal is still a bad deal. You still need to deal with the property once you get the MLO in place. So when should and when shouldn't you activate an MLO?

Here are some big-picture considerations:

1. What property type is right for you?
2. What financial data do you need to review?
3. What do the numbers mean?
4. Who will manage the property?
5. What (if any) repairs are needed?

The first thing you need to focus on when analyzing a deal is the property type. What I mean by "type" is the size, price, complexity, and experience level required. You want to grow your business, but you must be careful of the rate at which you grow. Don't take a deal you aren't equipped to handle. You need to know what is too much for your level of experience/real estate education. If you own two or three houses, you may not be ready for a 200-unit apartment complex, even if a seller accepts an MLO offer.

My suggestion is to obtain properties no more than 20 percent larger than the last one each time. If you own one house, then look at 10- to 20-unit apartment complexes. If you own a 50-unit complex, then go up to a 60-unit or, at most, a 75-unit deal. This will keep your growth in line with your level of experience.

Early in my career, I moved too fast, and it landed my company in an accounting nightmare. We didn't have experience with the management software to operate a 240-unit portfolio property we had just taken over, so we quickly bought a newer and much larger system. Then we realized we were inept at using this software, too. Our reporting and management were extremely difficult for a few months, and my team was miserable.

The lesson here: Go big as soon as you can but not too big too quickly.

VALUING A DEAL

There are several ways to determine the value a property. These are not specific to CSF or MLOs—these methods are used to value real estate in general. Keep in mind we must understand the true value of an asset to be able to make a creative offer. Here are the three most common valuation techniques:

1.   The income approach

2. The cost approach
3. The sales comparison approach

THE INCOME APPROACH

The income capitalization approach (income approach) is a method of valuing an income-producing asset with the basic idea that a property is worth some multiple of its revenues/cash flow. This is done by using a gross rent multiplier (GRM) or a cap rate (see chapter 8) applied to the NOI.

Gross Rent Multiplier = Property Price / Gross Rental Income

For GRM to be useful, it needs to be compared to the general GRM in the submarket (3–5 miles surrounding your asset). This can be determined in a form of comparable data such as sales prices or price per square foot. Once you know the GRM for your area, you can quickly calculate the value of a property. For every $1 of increase in income, you can increase the value of the asset by its GRM.

For example, if the GRM in a city is 10, then for every $1 you have in revenue, you have $10 in value. For every $1 that you can increase the revenue, you will increase the value of the GRM. In this case, it's $10 in value for every $1 in increased income. Therefore, renovating properties and improving operations is a great way to quickly increase value.

If a property has little to no revenue (distressed asset), you'll need to create a financial projection for the project.

THE COST APPROACH

This method is least used by the average investor in commercial real estate. I mention it here because it's an important concept to understand but not one you'll use in everyday analysis. The cost approach determines the value of a property by summing the land value and the depreciated value of any improvements.

The basic concept adds up all the costs of replacing existing buildings with brand-new ones (replacement cost). Now subtract the depreciated value of the old buildings from the replacement cost using comparable data from the market. This valuation technique is most often used by appraisers and is combined with the income and comparison sale approaches to create an average value.

USING THE INCOME APPROACH

Now that you have some definitions, I will be focusing on the first two, which are the income approach and the comparable sales approach for valuation. These are the main methods a lender will use to value a prospective property, and they are the best ways for you to start your evaluation of a property, too.

The income approach focuses on the value of a real estate investment based on its ability to produce income. The more cash flow a property produces, the more valuable it is. The less it produces, the less valuable it is. You need to start with the financial data from a property to begin your evaluation, and you can get this data directly from the broker or the seller. There are three things you will need to obtain:

1. Month-to-month profit and loss (T12)
2. Year-end profit and loss
3. Current rent roll

These are the three financial reports mentioned earlier that you will need in order to make an accurate assessment of the financial health of the property. These are also the same financials a lender wants to see if you refinance the property (seller financing) or originate debt to exercise your purchase option.

When you learn how to read these statements through practice, they will tell you the story of a property. Here are a few things I've learned to look for when viewing a property's financial statements:

1. High turnover costs (make-ready expense). This means either the tenants move in and out quickly (unstable tenant base), or the management spends too much in turn costs. If more than 6 percent of the tenant base is unstable, then management/rent collection will be difficult.
2. Water or gas utility expenses that have a large increase in a single month (leak).
3. Advertising costs that are more than $100 per door per year (may not be a desirable location).
4. Expenses per door should be in line with market average.
5. Lack of financial data altogether or disorganized data.

Once you have *current* financials on the property, you are ready to get started. Don't accept financial data from an owner or broker that is more than 90 days old. If a property is profitable and has been well run, the owner/broker will be quick and confident to give you the financial data. If the owner/broker is slow or gives you old data, then the asset is probably distressed in some way.

Let's take a closer look at valuing a property with the income approach.

STEP 1

Total all the property's income. This includes rent, late fees, and other income. This will give you *effective gross income*. In this approach, I'm not taking vacancy into account. I'm just working off what the property collected. If you want to factor in vacancy, you'll need to figure out the *gross scheduled rent* and then subtract vacancy from that. The numbers are the same in both formulas. Gross scheduled rent is calculated by assuming the property is 100 percent occupied at market rents. You would use the rent roll to determine this.

STEP 2

Now that we have the income for the property, we'll add all the property's expenses. This will include, but is not limited to, repairs, utilities, contract services, management fees, insurance, and taxes. This gives us our total expenses for the property. Do not include the debt service (loan payments) in this calculation.

STEP 3

Now you need to calculate the property's net operating income (NOI). NOI is calculated by taking the total income and subtracting the total expenses for the property. The NOI is cash flow only if you don't have any mortgage payment. If there is a mortgage payment, then that payment is made from the NOI. Here is a basic formula showing the math:

Total Income – Total Expenses = NOI
NOI – Mortgage Payment = Cash Flow

This gives you a quick snapshot of the financial viability of a deal. Does it cash flow? Again, you want to see a $100- to $150-per-door cash flow per unit for most apartment deals.

Capitalization rate or "cap rate" also helps you value a property and is one of the most common ways to determine value.

Cap Rate = NOI / Value (Sale Price)

Now that you know the formula, you can calculate the different values if you have these two variables. If you know the NOI and the sale price, you can determine your own valuation for the property. Here's another version of the same equation:

Value = NOI / Cap Rate

Cap rate can be slightly confusing. They are always in percentages, so an 8 cap would be .08. If you were to purchase a property for $1,000,000, then you would get $80,000 a year from this property ($1,000,000 x .08). In this example, it would take 12.5 years for the NOI to pay back the purchase price of the property ($1,000,000 / $80,000 = 12.5).

Something else to keep in mind is that cap rates typically move inversely to property value or price. The higher the value of the property, the lower the cap rate; the lower the value, the higher the cap rate. Brand-new, A-class apartment complexes can have cap rates of 4–6, whereas an older D-class asset in a bad neighborhood may have an 11–12 cap rate.

You might be thinking, "Who cares about these formulas? I'm going to get an MLO on the property. Why should I bother valuing the deal like this?" Even if you get an MLO, there is the "option" portion of an MLO. If your plan is to purchase the property at the end of the contract, a lender will use these calculations to value the deal. If the deal doesn't have the value you need, then you may be required to put down more cash at closing than you would like.

If you need cash to close the deal, you want to know as far in advance as possible—ideally before you even sign the MLO contract. What you don't want to happen is to have only a few months left in your contract, go to qualify for a loan to purchase the property and complete the option, and not have the value you need. In this case, you'd be scrambling around, trying to raise the cash to cover the difference, and time may run out on your MLO contract. If this happens, the seller has every right to keep your option money, and you would be out of that cash. Therefore, it's vital to know the value of the property long before you commit yourself to a contract.

CASH ON CASH

Cash on cash is another calculation that is part of the income approach. Here is the equation:

Cash on Cash = Cash Flow / Acquisition Cost

Acquisition costs are the expenses and money it takes to get to the closing, including the down payment. Cash on cash tells us the return on investment (ROI) the property will produce for the money it takes to close the deal. Mostly, this is the return you will receive on the down payment and closing costs. This comes into play more so when qualifying for a loan, rather than with an MLO, but you could also calculate cash on cash for the "option money" you put into an MLO deal.

Cash on cash comes into play if you plan to use a lender to help you purchase the property when you exercise the option. The lender will require you to put down a certain amount of the purchase price at closing, called the *down payment*. If you do not have the down payment money, you need to find partners to join you in the deal who will bring the cash you need at closing. This partner (or partners) will want to know what ROI they will receive on the cash they put into the deal. In a private investment such as this, most investors are looking for around 8–10 percent return on their money. If you need 20 percent down to get a loan and complete your purchase option, then you need to know how well the deal will service this 20 percent down.

Example:

$1,000,000 purchase price with a loan to value (LTV) of 80 percent

You need $200,000 down to get the loan.

If your deal produces $20,000 in cash flow, the cash on cash is 10 percent.

$200,000 / $20,000 = 10$

This is a simple concept but especially important in the long run. This cash on cash is how you will attract an investor to your deal if you need help with the down payment for a loan. If I were to come to you and say I needed you to invest in a deal with me and I'm going to give you a 3 percent return on your money, that's not very interesting. If you can't offer partners an attractive return, they won't be interested, and you may not be able to get the loan completed. This puts your option money at risk.

Some things to remember: Always use actual historical financial data to calculate these values. DO NOT USE PRO FORMA NUMBERS PROVIDED BY A REALTY AGENT.

Realtors may try and talk you into using pro forma numbers (best-case estimates) to value a deal. Don't do it. Use only real data from the property's operations over the last 12 months. Typically, a lender will use only historical data to value property for a loan. If you analyze your deal in any other way, you may not value it in the same manner as a lender.

CASH FLOWING

When analyzing a deal for the first time, consider your experience. If you are just getting started in the real estate investment business or you have fewer than fifty units, I strongly suggest you only do deals that are cash flowing on day one. You need your first deal to be a winner.

NOT CASH FLOWING

Don't take on a distressed asset unless you have some experience in these types of properties, or at least make sure you have a partner who has the experience. These deals can be diamonds in the rough or just rough. I've done both types. If you're ready to take on a distressed property, the MLO can be a great way to turn around the operations of a property and make it financially viable again. The biggest risk here is the option money you put up to get the contract in place.

Once you identify an owner who has a distressed deal, your analysis of their property will be different than if it is cash flowing. Using the formulas above will only tell you according to the income (or lack of income), if what the property produces will not support the option price. It's not rocket science. You need to value the deal with the comparable sales approach, which is explained in the next section, and by knowing your exit strategy. What I mean by "knowing your exit strategy" is that you need to be able to tell what the After-Repair Value (ARV) is, and what you plan to do with the property. After you fix the property up, you need to know it will be worth what you put into it, plus it must have an acceptable profit margin.

At that point, you need a plan to sell or exercise your option (MLO) and buy it yourself. If you plan to sell it, can you put a price on the property that covers all your repair and operational expenses that is still below the market value of the deal? You want to be able to sell a property below market value so you can attract qualified investors. You want to make money, but so does the next buyer, so don't get greedy with the price. You'll only be able to do this if you paid the right price to begin with.

The MLO and seller financing are great ways for doing reposition deals because you can mitigate much of the risk with this type of property by using this form of financing. Here are two suggestions if you are looking at a deal that needs lots of repairs and you don't have the cash to do them, or if the property is not breaking even with expenses currently.

The first suggestion is to use the option money for repairs. I never do an MLO deal or seller financing where there are lots of repairs and I must put down cash to get into the deal. I use the earnest money and/or the option money to get the repairs done. I explain to the owner/seller that the property needs extensive repairs. I am not interested in spending my cash on earnest money or option money to then have to come up with more cash out of pocket to complete the needed repairs to someone else's property. I offer to set up an escrow account (the same account for making payments for the property) and put the option money into that account. The seller will be able to see the money there, but it won't go to the seller. I will then use this money to fund the necessary repairs at the property. The seller can see you really do have the earnest money, and that should make them more comfortable with doing the deal with you. However, they won't be able to take control of the money. You will use it to make the repairs.

You should offer to allow the owner to approve withdrawals after they inspect the work you have already done. Once the owner is satisfied with the first round of repairs and approves the withdrawal, you then take some cash from the escrow account to do more repairs. This keeps the seller involved in the process of spending the option money for repairs to a property you didn't mess up in the first place. You may need to allow the owner to be a signer on the account so they'll be comfortable with this concept. You'll also need to explain to them that by doing the needed repairs, this creates value for them at their property. Even if you were to default in some way, they keep the repairs that were done, and they're still in a better situation than they were before you came along.

The second suggestion is to use the total income of the property to fund the repairs. What I'm suggesting here is that you negotiate to defer a few of the first payments. In this method, you take control of the property and use all the property's income to do the repairs, because you don't have to make a payment to the seller. This works best when the seller/owner has a lot of or total equity in the deal. You want to put off the first few payments so you can use most of the rents you collect for repairs to the property.

This is a great way to get unrentable units back in rent-ready condition. As you make each unit ready and rent them, you increase the amount of income the property produces each month. If you can put off the first 3–6 months' worth of payments, you'll give yourself more room to operate each month. If you choose either of these systems, you won't pay yourself while the property is not profitable. Only pay yourself once you get the property fully stabilized and cash flowing. You are working for free to build a property, but you will qualify for a bank loan or sell it later. If you try to take cash flow from an unstabilized property before it is truly profitable, you greatly increase your chances of failure. Put all collected income back into the property until it cash flows on its own!

VALUATION THROUGH OPERATION, NOT RENOVATION

Besides a great location, there is another great way to increase a property's value: more cash flow! An investment property's value is largely based on its income. The more money it makes, the more valuable it is. In basic terms, as a property's NOI increases, its value increases, too.

The only ways to increase the NOI is to increase revenue or cut expenses. Most people focus solely on renovating units and increasing rents. This works well in the expansion portion of the market cycle, but in the contraction and recession portion of a market cycle, the renovate-and-raise rent model can be strained. When times are more financially challenging, renters tend to be more price sensitive than quality sensitive. That nice fancy unit with the new paint and granite countertops may be great, but if tenants can't afford it, who cares how nice it is?

In down market cycle, it is best to create value through operation, not renovation. In the recession cycle, it's best to find deals that are just mismanaged, rather than deals that require a ton of work. Look for deals with high expenses that can be lowered quickly. Trying to force value by renovating a property as prices decline is what we call catching the falling knife.

As the market cycles through its phases from expansion to recession, you'll need to constantly update how you value deals. Don't just stick with one method and think it will work in all market cycles. It won't.

This reminds me of a deal I closed in April of 2010. I purchased a 44-unit apartment complex with 100 percent seller financing. Sound too good to be true? It was. The catch was, the seller financing was only for 90 days. I had to renovate the asset and qualify for a refinance within that time frame.

The backstory is, the seller was an elderly lady, and her husband had just died, leaving her with this 44-unit apartment complex. My attorney at the time brought me the deal. The lady was also a client of my attorney, so he knew her situation and the reputation I had for solving these types of problems. The lady had no debt on this asset, so she was able to offer 100 percent seller financing for a short amount of time. Unfortunately, her husband had left a fair amount of other debt that was now in default. She needed to divest of this asset quickly, but she also couldn't carry the debt for long, as she needed the cash to deal with other creditors. Hence the 90-day financing.

I negotiated the debt to be 100 percent of the sale price because the asset was financially distressed. The occupancy at the time of purchase was about 50 percent. Traditional lenders weren't interested in nonperforming assets like this one, but I saw the ultimate potential. I knew the asset was a good property; it had just been mismanaged. There was no reason for the low occupancy other than the seller had run out of money, and he stopped getting the units rent-ready when tenants moved out. I was sitting on a potential cash cow, and all I needed to do was get the units into good rental condition. Because the asset was in bad economic shape and the seller needed a quick turnaround (90 days), I decided to negotiate aggressively.

In my analysis of the asset, I realized this property could potentially create a lot of monthly cash flow if the occupancy stabilized and a permanent loan was in place. I created a pro forma for the deal. I looked at market rents for the area and figured out what the total revenue could be for this asset. I got comparable rents for this property by doing what property management calls a market survey. That's a fancy way of saying I called other apartment communities in the area and asked what they charged for renting similar units. Once I knew the rents in the area, I totaled up the number of units and floor plans I had and multiplied by 12 to get the annual income. I subtracted 10 percent for vacancy and bad debt. I knew the operating costs of this property would be about 40 percent of the rental revenue. Then I calculated my NOI and subtracted the debt service from that. What was left over was cash flow. Here's the math:

UNIT TYPE	1 BED/1 BATH	2 BED/1 BATH	3 BED/2 BATH	TOTAL
Market Rent	$700	$800	$1,000	
Number of Units	22	14	8	44
Monthly Rent	$15,400	$11,200	$8,000	$34,600
Annual Rent	$184,800	$134,400	$96,000	$415,200

I took the annual rent ($415,200) and subtracted 10 percent for vacancy ($4,152) to get the estimated annual income of $411,048.

I knew that when I had the property up and running properly, it should be producing about $411,000 a year after accounting for vacancy and uncollectable rent (10 percent). Next, I had to figure out my exit strategy. I had to calculate two exit strategies: one for the 90-day financing and one for the long-term hold after the initial 90 days.

Because I had seller financing, I had two great options for an exit strategy. I could refinance the property, or I could sell it. I opted to refinance and keep the asset because of the high cash-flow potential. I refinanced with a lower interest rate loan through a traditional lender. I also knew I had only 90 days to get this asset to where it needed to be for refinancing. I had to take occupancy from 50 to 90 percent or more within the next 90 days. To do this, I had to fully renovate and lease about twenty units in that same time frame. I had my work cut out for me, but with 100 percent seller financing, I didn't see that I had much to lose.

I set up the loan with the seller (through my attorney) to start on the first day of the following month. That way, I could collect rent from the existing tenants. I used the collected rent to fix up a few more units, and I leased those apartments quickly. The first of the next month came, and I collected rent from the existing tenants plus rent from the newly leased units. I used that money to fix up a few more apartments and leased them out, too. The third month came, and I had finished all the renovations with nothing but the rent I collected from the property. With a little creativity and some sweat equity, the apartment complex paid for its own renovations in under 90 days. At this point, you may be thinking, "Didn't you have a mortgage payment on this seller financing?" No, I did not. I negotiated *no payments* for the 90 days of seller financing. The seller did charge interest on the loan, but it was accrued and added to the loan balance that was due in full in 90 days. No sweat!

Now, there are two more points to discuss here: seasoning period and loan origination period.

Seasoning period is the length of time you need to own an asset before a lender will allow you to refinance based on a new appraisal and not the last purchase price. The lending environment has changed since the deal I've been talking about. Back then, I was able to refinance with a local lender based on the new appraisal or after-repair value (ARV). ARV is the value of the property after I fixed it up and stabilized the operations. Most lenders don't allow you to refinance a property and borrow against the ARV until you have owned the asset for at least 12 months (seasoning period). However, lenders have the ability to change this. They can and will make special allocations for certain borrowers and on certain properties, but it's a good general rule of thumb to hold on to the asset for 12–24 months when using a cash-out refinance exit strategy. Just to be safe.

The second point to discuss is the loan origination period. Once you apply for traditional financing, the lender usually requires 45–90 days to complete most commercial loans. I make this point because in my example I had 90-day financing but was also refinancing with a local bank to pay off the seller financing. The time frames don't line up.

I had 90-day financing, but the contingency was that I had to *qualify* for a loan to refinance within the 90 days. I didn't have to have the loan application process *completed* in 90 days. Our attorney wanted to make sure I could perform the renovations and stabilization of the asset and that I could get it to a level where a lender would underwrite it (in 90 days). I made an agreement with the attorney, allowing him to hold the new title in escrow. I had to resign documents that would allow the seller to immediately take back possession of the asset without a formal foreclosure process. This meant if I didn't get the bank to agree to refinance the deal within the 90-day seller financing window, I would have to give the property back to the seller within a 24-hour window. No questions asked.

On day 87 of 90 of my seller financing window, the property looked great! The units were renovated and most were rented. My plan to stabilize the asset had worked out perfectly. I even put in my loan application with a local bank I had a great relationship with. All was going exactly as planned, except I hadn't heard from the bank as to whether or not I qualified for the refinance. I had definitely lost a few hours of sleep the last few nights. Here I was with 3 days left, and I hadn't heard anything from the lender. But of course, I did hear from the attorney.

Day 87 was on a Thursday, and day 90 was going to fall on a Sunday. The attorney said, "Well, it was a good run. You did well, and we appreciate the condition the asset is in now, but you haven't qualified for your loan, and day 90 is this Sunday. Come in on Monday and we'll take the deed out of escrow. We'll take over the asset and its operations at that time." I agreed and set an appointment to visit his office the following Monday. The next afternoon, on Friday, the lender called and said I had qualified for the refinance. I had less than 5 hours left before I completely lost that deal. It was damn close!

COMPARABLE SALES APPROACH

This approach to valuing a deal considers the comparable sales (comps) in the area. You will look at what other people have paid for similar properties in the area and use that information to find the market value of your property. When you look at the sale of properties in a market to decide its value, you need to know whether or not you are looking at a comparable property. Consider the following:

1. Distance: Apartments need to be in the same submarket (within a 3- to 5-mile radius around your subject property).
2. Age: The comps should be built within 5–10 years of your property.
3. Size: Houses should be the same bed/bath and square footage. Apartments should be the same bed/bath and square footage of each unit type, but the total number of units should also roughly be the same. You wouldn't compare a 10-unit complex to a 150-unit complex.
4. Amenities: You should check to see if competing complexes have more or better amenities than your property. Make sure your property has similar amenities, such as a pool or laundry facility. In newer properties, you need to look for additional amenities such as a recreational facility or a business center. Do other comps offer free cable or Wi-Fi and yours does not? This makes a big difference in total property value.

A formal appraisal from a licensed appraiser is the only way to be sure of a property's value. You will likely have to do an appraisal before you get a loan on the deal and close your option on the property. Using these valuation techniques won't keep you from doing appraisals, but they will help keep you from spending money on one that you don't need in the first place.

If you find that a property passes your valuation, then you

want to pay for the actual appraisal, but not before you do your own homework on the property. The income approach will help you determine if the deal will make money or not. The comparable sale approach will help you place the deal into the surrounding market as far as value is concerned. You should use both.

In the introduction, I told you the first property I ever bought was a duplex in a bad neighborhood. I used only the income approach to value the deal, and that was a problem. I paid about $45,000 for the property, which sounded good at the time. I even qualified for a 30-year Fannie Mae mortgage. Each unit rented for about $400 a month, and my mortgage payment was around $375. So my cash flow for the two units was about $300–$400, depending on repairs for the month.

The cash flow sounded good to me, and I closed the deal. However, about 2 weeks after I bought the property, I realized all the other investors on the street had paid about $25,000 for similar properties. OOPS! I hadn't looked at recent sales in the area, and it cost me. Don't make the same mistake. Use both methods.

HOW TO AVOID MISTAKES

Here are a few other ways to avoid mistakes when analyzing deals.

KNOW YOUR MARKET

When you begin valuing a deal, you'll want to look very closely at the market surrounding your property. As you saw from my mistake, you can lose big if you don't know your market. I ended up okay only because I bought for cash flow, not for sale value. If I bet on selling at a profit, I would have gone into foreclosure with that deal.

UNDERSTAND OCCUPANCY

Find out the average occupancy of comparable properties in your area. If you look at an apartment deal and see that occupancy is 70 percent and you will cash flow at 85 percent, getting those units rented is a value play for this deal. If you look within a 3- to 5-mile radius and all the properties in the area are at 70 percent occupancy, then this is not a value play at all: it's the market! *Remember, you can rehab a property, but you cannot rehab a market.*

KNOW YOUR COMPETITION

Don't look at a property with two-bed units and then look at other properties with three-bed units and simply compare the rents. Other properties may charge more for a two-bed unit than you are, but if they have bigger units, then increasing your rent is not a value play. It will make you less competitive in the area. Compare price per square foot (total rentable square feet divided by the rent) to make sure you are competitive with your rents.

KNOW THEIR AMENITIES

The more amenities you have, the more you can charge for rent. Make sure when you compare rents you also consider the value of your competitor's amenities. If they have a pool and you don't, they can charge more in rent for a similarly sized unit.

KNOW THE NEIGHBORHOOD

You should never buy a property in an area that you don't understand. This is easy to say but hard to do. I suggest you really get to know an area before doing business there. Low-income areas tend to be harder to manage, but high-income areas tend to be more expensive. You'll need to find a balance between what you can afford to get into and what you can afford to deal with. An MLO may allow you to get into a deal easier than if you bought it outright, but you must keep in mind that you still have to deal with it day in and day out. If you wouldn't spend the night on your property, then you probably shouldn't own or manage it.

GETTING THE CASH BACK

This is the final concept we'll discuss for valuing a deal. I've already said that in an MLO deal, I like to get my earnest money back from operations of the property in the first half of the contract time. The faster I get my money out of harm's way, the more value I put on the deal.

When you look at the value of a property, you need to look at the terms by which you will take control of the deal. The agreement you strike with the seller can affect the value as much as anything else. Try to figure out how many months it will take to cash flow back your option money. If their answer is that you won't get it back or that it may take most of the contract time to recover your money, then you need to reduce the value of that deal considerably.

In general, the terms can make or break a deal. You may have a great property that cash flows a lot of money, but if the seller will only accept an MLO offer contingent upon them getting almost all of the income, then it's not a good deal, regardless of the property. Likewise, if you have a deal that makes less income but the seller defers a year's worth of payments or doesn't require any option money at all, then the value is higher.

POINTS TO REMEMBER

Most people think building a real estate business or portfolio consists of driving around and looking at deals, meeting realtors, and high-profile closings. An exceedingly small percentage of your time will be spent doing these tasks. Money in real estate is made on spreadsheets, not at the closing table.

Finding deals is about deal analysis. Deal analysis is about long hours in front of a computer, looking at financial statements and creating pro formas. Sound boring? It is, but it pays.

ACTION ITEMS

Deal analysis is about deal flow. Keep analyzing three deals a week.

Keep networking for partners and investors.

Find deals to analyze online. Realtor websites are a great place to find properties you can analyze. You will likely need to sign a confidentiality agreement in order to download the info. Once you get the financial data, practice your deal analysis skills. Repeat until you are extremely comfortable with this process. Then start reaching out to realtors to establish relationships.

CHAPTER 10

MAKING OFFERS

The number one thing you must keep in mind when making a creative offer is to CREATE VALUE! I've seen many people make offers for CSF that never get accepted because they violate this one rule. Make sure the offer isn't written in such a way that it's one-sided in your favor. Protect yourself and your interests but still create value for the seller.

THE SPY TECHNIQUE

SPY stands for seller, property, you. This is the order in which you should approach making a creative offer.

> ➤ The seller's problems
> ➤ The property's problems
> ➤ Your problems

First, determine the problems the seller may have. Do they even know they may have a problem? Begin your deal analysis by gathering as much info as possible on the owner's motivation to sell. Money is not always the reason. Sometimes a seller believes the only way to solve their real estate problems is by selling. Solve the seller's problems first.

Second, find out what the property needs. Deferred maintenance? Renovations? Is it mismanaged? Once you've determined what's wrong with the property, you can craft an offer to help mitigate the assets' distress while minimizing risk for yourself.

Third, what do you need? This is the least valuable point in the negotiation for CSF or an MLO. Most people make the mistake of reversing the order of SPY and try to solve their own problems first. They tackle the asset issues next, and then as an afterthought, they see if their offer is a fit for the sellers' needs. This is a surefire way to NOT get your offers accepted. A willing seller is crucial to any good deal. Following SPY when creating offers will dramatically increase your offer acceptance rate.

GATHER THE DATA

When you first start working with an agent or seller, you need to do as much research as possible. This mostly includes simply talking to them and asking questions. Why are they selling? What do they want? What is the real motivation for selling? Do they need the cash for the sale right now?

I ask the same question in several different ways. You must do this to get the seller to open up and tell you the truth about their motivation to sell. When you understand their motivation, you'll be able to make an offer to solve their problems and decide how much time and effort you want to spend trying to close the deal.

A highly motivated seller may not actually be the best fit for CSF. I know that sounds backward, but it isn't. If a seller is extremely motivated, it could mean they need the cash right then and there. If this is the case, they're a lot less likely to give you financing. They will want a traditional sale with cash at closing. Don't waste too much time and energy trying to close a deal that isn't a fit for CSF. This will lead to frustration.

If a seller has a large amount of equity in the property or no mortgage at all, then seller financing may be a better fit. In this scenario, you take possession of the deal and become the owner of record. If you plan to do a lot of repairs and renovation to the property, the money and time you spend will be more secure if you're the actual owner.

LETTER OF INTENT

For most offers, I suggest using a letter of intent (LOI), which is a letter stating how you plan to buy the property and under what terms. The reason for using this instead of making your offer directly with a contract is to save time and money during your negotiation. Remember, you need to have a local attorney create any documents, and that process costs money.

The LOI is a way to begin the negotiation for free. Make the CSF offer and see if the seller is even interested before you spend money. The LOI is not a binding agreement and only *states* your offer. You don't need an attorney to draft this, as it is not a legal document. I have included a sample in this section.

When making an offer for CSF, follow the age-old acronym KISS: *Keep It Simple Stupid.*

A confused mind says no, so stay high level with this letter. This is not a contract. All the details of the offer need to be omitted for several reasons:

1. The seller may not understand the structure of a master lease or seller financing.
2. You will want a chance to explain/sell the offer.
3. You may need to educate the agent or seller about the offer.
4. People are lazy and don't want to read a document that looks confusing with lots of complicated text.

Write the LOI so it contains only the major points. For example, if it's for seller financing, you may state the price, state that the seller will carry back financing, and the basic terms such as interest rate, down payment, and the time period for the loan. If you want to negotiate the down payment to be used for repairs instead of giving it to the seller or use interest-only payments for a while to get repairs done, leave that out of the initial offer. Once you get the seller's attention and a response to the LOI, then you can set up a time to talk details with the seller or agent, or both.

CONVERSATION WITH SELLER AND AGENT

In your conversation with the agent/seller, you want to enthusiastically explain why the offer is valid, why it's good for the seller and agent, and why they should do business with you. If you were to put all of that into an initial offer, it would be too long and no one would read it.

Make the initial statement to the realtor explaining how you plan to do business with this seller, and then push for a meeting or phone call with them. It's helpful to get the agent on the phone as well. If they feel left out, it will not work in your favor. You also put the seller at ease when you encourage them to have their counsel present. Once you set up a meeting/discussion, you can then use that time to pitch the offer. Be ready to do the following, and remember you likely have only one shot at this, so be prepared.

1. Fully explain the nature of the offer (CSF, MLO, debt partner, etc.).
2. Explain how this structure works.
3. Explain why it's a benefit to the seller (what problem does it relieve for them?).
4. Explain how you plan to pay the agent (equity, share cash flow, etc.).
5. Explain how you plan to deal with the property itself.
   A. Use your business plan for the property, including the estimates you received from your contractors.
   B. Hit them up for the down payment to be used for the repairs.
   C. Discuss the number of repairs needed and the time frame to get them done.
   D. Discuss your plan for management and how it's different than what they've been doing.
   E. Back up all this information with statistics you've gathered from the market, contractors, and local managers.
   F. KNOW YOUR NUMBERS!
6. Discuss your legal counsel and how they have/will create all the documents, ensuring they are fully legal in your state. Offer to let their attorneys create or review them.
7. Discuss your exit strategy and how it will benefit the seller.

A. Do you plan to refinance with a lender once the property is stabilized and pay the seller/realtor in full?
B. Do you plan to fix and flip the property? Show stats that support appreciation in the market in a 3–5 mile radius around the property.
C. Will you bring the seller on as a full partner?
D. *Remember, the options are limited only by your imagination.*

As you can see, making a compelling offer for creative financing is not as simple as most people would like it to be. (I never said this would be easy.) Use the LOI and then be ready to put on your sales/negotiation hat! If a seller or agent doesn't respond favorably to your initial offer, I suggest asking this one question as soon as you get a no.

What is it about this offer that's not a fit for you (or your client)?

This will serve two functions. First, you will have a chance to reopen the negotiation if the seller/agent gives you a reason such as price or terms. These can be changed. Second, this will give you feedback that you may be able to incorporate into a future offer. You may lose this one, but if you learned something along the way, then it's a success.

I usually make an offer once, and if I get a no, I will gently try one more time. If I still get a no, then I walk away. It's better to get a polite no than to damage a relationship with an agent or seller by being too aggressive in your pitch. This leads us back to the reason for the LOI.

WHY YOU MAKE OFFERS IN WRITING

You make an offer in writing for the noes, not the yeses. If an offer is accepted, then you get your attorney involved to create the documents. If you get a no, the seller or agent still has something in writing to put in their file for the future. Many deals that go under contract never close. The seller may accept a different offer, believing that it is better, only to have it fall out of contract and never close. The seller or agent may need to pull out your old offer and reconnect with you.

In late 2010, I made my first offer on a larger apartment complex. It was a 152-unit deal with an LOI. After a few weeks, the agent replied, stating the seller had accepted another offer. I moved on and forgot about the deal. A little over a year later, I got a call from the same agent, even though I had not spoken to them in all that time.

Another buyer couldn't gather the money together to qualify for financing and purchase the property. This buyer wasted almost a year of the seller's time trying to close this deal! The agent had kept my LOI in a file this entire time, and when the contract fell through, I got a call. The seller now realized what I had told them was right all along: the property would have trouble qualifying for a loan unless operational changes were made. They realized I was right and wanted to talk.

My partner and I raised the funds needed for a 25 percent down payment, and the seller gave us total financing. We didn't need a bank to do the loan because the seller used the 25 percent cash we gave them to pay off the first mortgage. This allowed them to give us financing. The terms were good, and our exit strategy was to manage it with our team for about a year, straighten out the operations, and then refinance for a traditional loan and pay off the seller in full at the time of the refinance. We accomplished our mission, and it was possible only because the initial offer was in writing. You never know when a current no will turn into a future YES!

Here is an example of an LOI for reference:

Letter of Intent

RE: [Property Name Here]

Current Owner:

Please find outlined below the general terms and conditions under which (**Your Company**) would be willing to purchase the above referenced Property ("Property"). This letter will serve as a nonbinding letter of intent between the owner of record ("Seller") (**Your Company**) and _____ or its Assignee ("Buyer").

Let this letter serve as our expression of intent to purchase the above-referenced property under the following terms and conditions:

PROPERTY: [Property Name and Address Here]

1. **PRICE:** [Start with the total price you are offering]
2. **OFFER:** [Put offer type here such as MLO, CSF, partnership etc.]
3. **TERMS:** [Briefly describe the terms of the agreement]
4. **EARNEST MONEY DEPOSIT:** A refundable Earnest Money Deposit in the amount of $_____ will be deposited with the escrow agent within three (3) business days after signing the Purchase Agreement.
5. **INSPECTION PERIOD:** Purchaser shall have forty-five (45) days from the date of execution of formal contract to perform inspections and examine the records of the Property. If, for any reason, during this inspection period, Purchaser shall find the Property unsuitable, the Purchaser, by written notice to Seller, shall have the right to

declare this Letter and any Contract of Sale based hereon null and void and receive a refund of any Earnest Money that has been deposited.

6. **PURCHASE AGREEMENT:** Both parties will strive to execute a mutually acceptable Purchase Agreement or Acceptable Contract within 15 days after the execution of this Letter of Intent. The date of completion of the signed purchase agreement shall be the "Effective Date."

7. **BROKERAGE FEES:** [Discuss how to get the agent paid here]

8. **CLOSING DATE:** The Closing will occur on or before sixty (60) days after the Effective Date. Should constraints dictate additional time, an additional 30-day extension shall be available upon written request from Purchaser. Such written requests shall be made prior to the target Closing Date.

The above represents the general terms and conditions of the proposed transaction. The exact terms and conditions will be contained in a mutually acceptable Contract. Should the above proposal be acceptable to you, please execute your signature below and **(your company)** will begin preparation of the Purchase Agreement. Thank you for your consideration, and we look forward to the opportunity to work with you on this transaction.

PURCHASER:

BY: _____

NAME: _____

TITLE: _____

SELLER:

BY: _____

NAME: _____

TITLE: _____

POINTS TO REMEMBER

Solve problems. That is the number one way to get a CSF offer accepted. A good deal usually starts with a motivated seller. Sellers can be motivated for many reasons. Sometimes their motivation is obvious; other times, it's not so clear. Do as much fact-finding as possible before making an offer. Try to discover the pain points a seller may have. Once you know what truly motivates the seller (you might be surprised how often it's not money), you can begin to properly analyze the deal and create an offer that will get accepted.

Don't be afraid to make an offer that is low, but don't damage a relationship with a realtor over it. If you are working with a realtor, you'll want to get them on board with a low offer before you make it.

ACTION ITEMS

Make three offers.

Find three assets that can be "fixed" with a little help from the seller, and make one creative offer per property. Use the SPY technique to decide how the offer will solve the issues you've found, and submit an LOI. If there is a realtor involved, discuss the offer before you submit it.

Remember that the LOI is just a "back of the napkin" offer— it's not a contract. You don't have anything to lose at this point in the buying process, so don't overthink the situation. Just make three offers.

CHAPTER 11

DUE DILIGENCE

Due diligence (DD) for a CSF deal goes beyond the physical property itself. The type of creative financing you get will dictate how you conduct your DD. Start with the seller and the documents behind the deal.

OVERALL CHECKLIST FOR DUE DILIGENCE

This first section will cover DD for all CSF deals, and I'll cover MLOs in the next section.

MORTGAGE

The first item to request from the seller is the mortgage information. This is crucial if you are doing an MLO. A seller cannot give you interest in a property they don't have. If a seller has only 2 years left on an existing mortgage, you don't want to sign an MLO for 5 years. They are giving you 3 years that technically don't exist.

The seller can refinance the deal (hopefully) at the end of the 2 years, but if that doesn't go as planned, your MLO may become worthless. If you plan to do seller financing on a property and you find the seller has a mortgage in place, don't do the deal. A seller can't finance a deal to you when they still have a mortgage in place.

Don't get me wrong. I'm not saying that this isn't done. It's done all the time, but it's not a good idea. The seller can't give you title to the property because they don't have one to give you—the lender has the title. When a seller gives you financing and has financing in place, this is known as a "wrap" or "subject to" financing. You are wrapping your mortgage around the existing mortgage, or you are taking over the property "subject to" the existing financing.

I don't care for either of these situations personally. It can trigger what is known as a "due on sale" clause that is in the lender's mortgage with this seller. It states that if the property is "sold," the proceeds are due immediately to the lender. Your "wrap" financing can trigger the lender to call the entire loan due immediately, and your interest in the property will become null and void. The seller will then have to pay off the loan or go into foreclosure.

Most investors will tell you that if you are making the payments to the lender, they will turn a blind eye to the situation. They may, but it's still too risky. If you want to do this type of financing, I suggest you try to negotiate as little of a down payment as you can, and use the existing loan to support your negotiation. If you do put money down, then try to recover the cash back through the income of the property ASAP. You will want to get it back in at least half the time of the CSF contract.

If you still want to do a "wrap" or "subject to," then I suggest calling the lender and telling them you're going to do this type of financing. If they put in writing that it's acceptable, then go for it. If they don't give you permission and you do it anyway, then you're responsible for any negative consequences.

PROPERTY

You'll want to do a full inspection of the entire property as if you are going to buy it and pay all cash. Just because you may be getting a master lease or seller financing doesn't mean you should slack in your physical DD. You will be operating the property, and your cash flow will be contingent upon how well the property runs. If you don't do a full inspection and find major repairs that need to be done after you complete the takeover, it will be your problem. Do a thorough inspection so you know what you are getting into. You don't want to see your cash flow drained away by unexpected repairs.

Walk every unit during your inspection. I can't stress this enough. Don't let the owner or current management keep you from any of the units, no matter what the excuse is. The unit you don't go into will be the one that is totally trashed!

Here are a few items to look for when doing your walk-through:

1. Exterior of building
   A. Moisture damage/wood rot
   B. Obvious drainage issues
   C. Roofing
   D. HVAC unit (old is bad)
2. Inside the units, check:

A. Paint
B. Carpet
C. Appliances
D. HVAC
E. Electrical panel
F. Lights and fixtures

In general, you want to examine the age and condition of these items.

FREE INSPECTIONS

When I got started in the multifamily business, I didn't have much cash to pay for inspections, so I brought my contractors with me when I did my DD walk-throughs. Don't forget, you can trade work for free estimates. Use the contractor bids as part of your game plan when going forward with the deal.

After each contractor turns in their bids, you'll know what needs to be done and how much it will cost. With this information, you can then create a business plan to present to the seller, helping them make the decision of whether or not to give you CSF. This will also give you leverage for negotiating the agreement and the terms.

DUE DILIGENCE ON THE OWNER

I suggest doing some research on the owner or seller of any property. Remember, CSF is not just financing but also a "partnership" of sorts. You and the seller will be doing business together over the term of the loan or agreement.

Do an internet search on the seller or their company. See if you find any previous or pending legal action, including lawsuits. Do you see any foreclosures or judgments against them? If you find anything like this, you may not want to get involved.

Past issues may represent a pattern. If your seller is sued or goes into foreclosure, it's not likely to involve you directly, but your contract may become null and void due to a senior loan or lawsuit. Your only remedy is to sue the seller yourself. By doing some research on the seller, you can skew the odds in your favor.

TAXES AND CODE ENFORCEMENT

I highly suggest contacting the code enforcement office local to your CSF property. See if there are any outstanding code violations against the property. If there are, then find out what the remediation would be.

Make sure the property taxes are current. Call the county tax assessor's office to confirm, or have the seller provide you with proof of current payment.

INSURANCE

You may or may not need to get insurance. If you do an MLO or partner with a seller, you will not need to get insurance on the property. If you are doing seller financing and you take possession of the property title, you'll want to get your own insurance policy. If you are keeping the seller's insurance in place, you'll want to get a copy of the policy as part of your DD inspections.

Make sure the insurance is current and in place. If you do an MLO, then you want to be listed on the owner's policy as an "additional insured." You can request this directly from the insurance company; you don't have to go through the owner to do this.

Being listed on the policy shows you have an interest in the property. It doesn't alter the coverage, but it does keep you in the information loop. It keeps you notified that the property is covered; if the policy lapses or is canceled, you will know that, too. As we discussed earlier, you should make payments to the insurance (taxes and mortgage) from your third-party escrow account, as this is an additional layer of protection for you.

CLEAR TITLE

Another level of DD and security you can put in place is to have an attorney do a title search on the property prior to the execution of your CSF agreement. The purpose is to find out if there are any liens against the property the seller has not disclosed to you. This could be a "journeyman's lien" or a lien placed by an unpaid contractor. This could also be any form of legal judgment against the seller, such as unpaid taxes. This list is endless, so have your attorney check out the title.

PHYSICAL INSPECTION

This is usually a good place to start. Assuming you don't have to travel too far to walk the entire property, I'd start the DD process here. When you do a property inspection, you want to examine the entire property, including all of the units. ALL OF THE UNITS! Don't let the realtor or manager keep you from entering any unit on the property. If you can't get into a unit on the day you conduct your physical inspection, then set a time to come back and visit the units you didn't get into.

I've had to threaten to cancel an offer because I was not given access to a unit on a property. The management kept giving me excuses as to why I couldn't enter the unit.

I made this the seller's problem by telling them if their management didn't give me access to the unit, I'd be canceling my offer. The owner got involved, and we found out why I was not being given access. The unit had had a fire and was in bad shape. The manager charged the owner for repairs to the unit that were never completed. The owner was under the impression that the job was completed, but it was not.

This was the seller's problem, and I got a discount on the price. If I had closed the deal without getting access to the unit, it would have become my problem. If you aren't skilled in the physical repair aspect of this business, I suggest paying an inspector to do the walk-through. If you pay an inspector, I suggest you walk with them as they conduct the inspection. This will give you an opportunity to get to know the property and to learn what professional inspectors look for. You can get a property condition report from an inspector, but there is no replacement for seeing it firsthand.

As you conduct a physical inspection, keep in mind you will likely be responsible for the condition of this property once you enter the MLO. You will need to do repairs and handle deferred maintenance with the income the property produces. Deferred maintenance and repairs can kill a budget, so be realistic when you do your DD walk-through. Taking care of old repairs and bringing a property back to good condition is a great way to bring value to a deal, or to get a seller to accept an MLO offer. However, you want to make sure the property can financially support the repair cost.

Here are some areas to examine when doing a property inspection:

1. General condition of the property. Pretend you are a renter about to lease a unit. What sort of "feeling" does the condition of the property give you? Would you want to live there?
2. Roofs. These can be awfully expensive to replace. Check the roof condition of each building. If you have bad roofs, you will never get control of your maintenance expenses.
3. Siding. Look at the exterior of the buildings. If the property has a wood structure, check for rot. If you see a lot of wood rot, such as on siding or balconies, this can be expensive.
4. Appliances. Are they new or old? Appliances can determine whether a unit is rented or not. Old appliances make a unit much less desirable to a good tenant and will need to be replaced.
5. Landscape. Landscaping is where your curb appeal begins. Good landscaping can also help prevent crime and vandalism. This is not something that can be statistically proven, but I've found that if you let the landscaping get out of control, the surrounding neighborhood will treat the property accordingly. There's less loitering and crime when a property is taken care of.
6. HVAC. Your heating and air-conditioning units need to be assessed for age and condition. There have been

recent changes to regulations regarding the type of new HVAC systems that can be sold, and they don't tend to be compatible with older models. My point is, with these new regulations, a repair may turn into a full replacement if you need new parts that aren't compatible with older models. If you see that the HVAC systems are older, plan for a higher replacement budget.

7. Plumbing and electrical. This is an area in which you can incur some high costs, and it's also the hardest to inspect in a general walk-through. You'll want a professional to look at these systems for you.

Tip: I bring in my electrician and plumber when I do a property walk-through. They look at these systems for me, and they do it for free. The deal is that if they give me an idea about the condition of these systems and do the inspection for free, I guarantee them future work at the property. I also do this with my roofer.

LEASE AUDIT

This is the second part of a property inspection. You'll want to review the leases the owner/management has on file to verify the data they gave you when you made the offer. If you're doing a lease audit on a small property or a house, this is quite simple. If you're doing an audit on a larger apartment complex, then you may want to do a sample audit instead.

I suggest inspecting every third lease. If you find discrepancies, you'll need to go back and do every file. In a lease audit, you're checking to see if the lease the tenant signed matches the rent roll you were given when you made your initial assessment of the property. Look at the amount of rent on the lease. Does it match? Has the management or owner given any concessions, such as free rent or discounts that you weren't aware of? Look at the move-in dates and lease term to make sure they match. If there is ever a dispute with a tenant, the lease with their signature is what holds up, not what the seller told you. This is why it's important to review leases—to make sure they're legitimate and signed by a real person.

FINANCIAL AUDIT

By now, you've received the financial statements (T12) for the property. Now it's time to make sure the data is real. This rarely happens, but people can create a set of financials to represent whatever they want. Income numbers can be completely falsified, so you need to request a property tax return. If the person files the property tax return as their own, they may not want to give you all this information. Request that they pull out the property portion of their return and give you that.

Another way of proving a property's income is to see a bank statement showing the deposits have been made for the property each month. Your goal here is to verify the property is putting the same amount of money in the bank that the seller is telling you it collects. I've never found an owner who creates a false set of books to sell a property, but it can be done, so I always verify the income with a tax return or bank statement. This DD step must be completed before you give the seller any earnest or option money.

MANAGEMENT DUE DILIGENCE

You'll want to interview the management at the property, assuming there is any. Your goal is to decide if you want to keep the current management and find out if they even plan to stay. Sometimes management will quit when a property is taken over by a new owner. This should be determined early in the DD process to give you ample time to plan for any upcoming changes.

Plan to conduct a formal interview with the main management company, as well as with each individual who works on the property. You'll want to discuss their salaries and bonus structure. You want them to be paid well but not too much. Also, find out if the property is under- or overstaffed. Remember, properties are often overstaffed, and reducing the payroll can be a value play for the property.

Do a full review of management policies and leasing practices, including how they screen tenants. In one case, I found a low-income property where the owner hired a local management company to run it. The management company normally operated nice, new, A-class properties. The management set a high screening requirement—too high for the tenants at that level of property. They were running it as if it were one of their usual properties and were screening low-income tenants in the same manner. The occupancy was dropping sharply because they required too high of a credit score for the average tenants in that area. As usual, the owner was the one who paid the price in the end. Make sure your management leases and operates according to the asset class for that property.

Also, ask the manager on-site about unpaid contractors. Ask

them how the property's relationships are with local contractors. I've found that sometimes managers are slow to pay contractors, or they have many outstanding invoices with contractors and suppliers for the property. Unpaid contractors will not show up to do work for that property, and they tend not to care or notice when a property changes hands. All they remember is that they weren't paid. The relationships and reputation a property has with its suppliers and contractors tells you a lot about how current management has been running the property.

My last MLO deal on a large property came with $50,000 in unpaid invoices from local contractors. These were unpaid under the old management company. I knew about these when I went into the deal, but had I not known about the unpaid invoices beforehand, it would have been a nasty surprise.

SELLER DUE DILIGENCE

Check on your seller as much as possible before entering an MLO with them. I'm not suggesting you hire a private detective to sit outside their house, but I am suggesting you at least do an internet search and see what you find. You want to look for bankruptcies or any other form of pending legal action. If you find bankruptcies or past legal troubles, you may want to be careful about entering into an agreement with them.

You might be surprised at how much information is in the public domain. It pays to check out the seller. You may be getting a good deal with the MLO, but you're also making an investment in their property with your time, energy, and possibly money. Don't invest blindly. Find out whom you are doing business with.

TITLE CHECK

It's a good idea to pay an attorney to do a title check on the property. This usually isn't that expensive. A title check proves the owner is the owner on record and that they have the right to enter the MLO contract with you. Again, I've never known a seller to try to and rip someone off like that, but it is good to be safe. Trust, but verify.

A title check also shows any outstanding liens on the property. This lets you know if there are unpaid contractors who may have placed a lien against the property, liens the seller may not have admitted, or liens they may not have even known about.

CODE ENFORCEMENT

I like to call the local code enforcement office to check for code violations on the property. This office will tell you if there are any outstanding violations. This is important because if a property is not up to code, the owner is responsible for bringing it up to code at their expense. As the holder of the MLO, you aren't the owner on record, but you may have to deal with code violations that could unexpectedly cut into cash flow.

LEGAL REVIEW

This is arguably the most important DD item. You'll need to have a local attorney create or review all documents pertaining to the deal, especially the MLO contract. It's particularly important to have an attorney review the documents (one who is licensed in the state in which the deal is conducted). Each state has differing laws that govern such contracts. Therefore, you want an attorney who is *local to the deal* to review or create the documents.

One of the biggest risks of doing an MLO deal is that you are not the owner on record. The owner may be sued or go into foreclosure, and you would be relatively powerless to stop this. I suggest having your attorney create clauses in the master lease document that penalizes the seller if this were to occur. These clauses are called remedies. They won't stop the legal action against the owner of record, but they will give you the right to act against the seller if they are sued or go into foreclosure.

Your attorney will give you the actual verbiage, but what the remedies should do is to make the seller repay the option money to you immediately if the title becomes encumbered (through no fault of your own) during the period of your master lease. If the property title becomes encumbered, then this verbiage will give you the right to take legal action against the seller to recover your option money.

I strongly suggest involving legal counsel in each deal you do because the risks can change. There is little you can do to totally avoid risk, which is why you need to be counseled for each individual deal.

DUE DILIGENCE FOR THE MLO

Conducting accurate DD on a property and seller are just

as important as analyzing the financial data. You'll want to do your DD as if you were buying the property and paying all cash. If you were about to spend that much of your hard-earned money, then I imagine you'd want to know what you were buying.

The DD for an MLO deal is no different. This section will show you how to conduct DD on all items from the seller to the existing mortgage on the property. Your DD into the MLO process is a crucial part of the deal.

ONCE THE OFFER IS ACCEPTED

Once the offer is accepted, then the real DD starts. My suggestion is to do as much "free" DD as possible before you start spending money. What is "free" will be different for each deal, so start by making a list of DD items to be accomplished, ranging from the least to the most expensive.

In some cases, walking the property and looking at the condition of the area may be the cheapest step to start with, but if the property is in another market or state, then that may need to be placed further down the list. Keep in mind you want to spend as little money as possible until the offer process is much further along and the deal is more likely to close.

RECORD THE CONTRACT

The MLO contract must be filed with the court system at the time of your signing. This is called recording the document. You will add the MLO contract to the title documents in the legal system. The point in doing this is to "cloud" the title.

By recording the document, anyone who pulls the title to this property will find your MLO contract. This prevents the seller from selling the property without you knowing it. When the next buyer/attorney researches the property's deed, they'll find the contract and it will prevent the sale. If the document is not recorded, it will not be found. This is an extremely important part of the MLO process and protects your interest in the deal. This is yet another reason to have a local attorney involved in every step of an MLO deal.

LOAN REVIEW

Before you sign the MLO contract or give any option money, have the seller disclose all the loan documents as part of your DD work. A seller cannot give interest in a property they don't have. When you review the loan documents, look at the time frame for the loan. If a seller has a loan for 2 years, they can't give you a master lease for 4 years. This would be giving you interest in a deal they don't have.

Loans do renew but not always. Don't let the seller give you a time frame for your MLO that extends past the terms of the loan. If the bank doesn't renew the loan, then the seller must refinance elsewhere. If they don't, the property will go into foreclosure, which overrides your MLO contract and you will lose the deal. You also need to look at the term of the loan and make sure it gives you a long enough time period to do what you need to accomplish, such as working on renovations.

Also, look at the terms, such as the monthly payment and escrow accounts. Make sure the numbers you originally analyzed are the real numbers. Defeasance for prepayment penalties is something else to keep in mind when looking at loan documents. Some loans have prepayment penalties if the loan is paid off early. If you plan to exercise your option to purchase and pay off an existing loan as an exit strategy, this may be an important factor. A prepayment penalty has to be paid from the owner's profits, or it could raise the cost/price of the deal. This is something to negotiate into the option price if the penalty exists.

WHEN YOU SHOULDN'T DO A MASTER LEASE OPTION

Here are some situations you may encounter in the DD process that are major red flags and that indicate you should not do an MLO deal:

1. A property won't ever cash flow. Some properties will never make money simply because the seller paid too much. Don't assume someone else's problem unless the work will be profitable.
2. The property is too big for you. Don't do a deal that puts you on a property that is far above your level of experience
3. The seller doesn't have a clear title. Don't do an MLO with a seller who cannot show you a clear title. They may not have the right to enter into the MLO with you.
4. The terms of the existing loan are too short. Don't do an MLO if the underlying loan term doesn't give you enough time to complete your exit strategy.
5. You can't identify a clear-cut exit strategy. Don't go into a deal when you don't have a great plan to get out of it. Identify your exit strategy early in the analysis process.

POINTS TO REMEMBER

Begin your DD with the seller. Why are they selling? What is their plan B if they don't accept your offer? How can your offer solve their problems? If cash is the only reason a seller is willing to sell, CSF probably won't work. Look for distressed owners.

Have an attorney clear the title before executing a CSF contract. You need to make sure the seller has the right to commit to the offer.

Do a full inspection on any property if you are getting a CSF. Act as if you are paying cash or getting a loan.

> ➤ Walk every unit.
> ➤ Inspect all financial data.
> ➤ Perform a lease audit of every tenant.
> ➤ Conduct all legal DD.

ACTION ITEMS

See the DD checklist at the end of chapter 14 to familiarize yourself with the standard items of the DD process. I didn't provide an explanation for every item on the list. If you don't know what something is, now is a good time to look it up.

CHAPTER 12

NEGOTIATING THE DEAL

Negotiation is one of the most profitable skills a business owner can have. Without the ability to negotiate the terms of an agreement, you will fall short when trying to create a winning deal.

In this chapter, I'm going to teach you how to negotiate a CSF offer, but I highly suggest you take your negotiation education further than this book. I could write volumes on this subject and still not cover it all. This is a skill you must practice and develop over time.

GATHER THE DATA

All good negotiations start with information. You'll want to gather as much info on the property and owner's situation as possible.

THE PROPERTY

Gather as much information on the property and all its problems as you can. Here are a few areas to look for:

1. Needed repairs
2. High payoff amount
3. Existing mortgage
4. Bad management
5. Low occupancy
6. Low or no cash flow
7. General property distress

Get as much of this information as you can by talking to the seller or their agent. You can always come back and renegotiate later if need be, but you want to do as much negotiation as possible up front.

Once you have some of this information, you can use this to negotiate items in your agreement. If the property requires a lot of expensive repairs, then negotiate to use the down payment or option money for the repairs. Remember, you don't want to spend a bunch of money to get into the deal and then spend more money to get it stabilized.

Negotiate with the seller to use any down payment cash for the rehab. Don't just give the seller the cash to hold for you. Set up a third-party escrow account to hold the money. Allow the seller to approve draws against the account as the work is being completed. You can also negotiate the first few payments to be interest-only or deferred altogether. Use your contractors to get an accurate cost estimate for the needed repairs. Once you know the cost of the repairs, you can then ask for an equal amount of payments to be deferred or to be interest-only.

When negotiating, don't make up numbers you would like to have, such as X amount of payments interest-only. You must be able to explain your numbers when requesting a concession. In this example, you'd use the repair costs that are backed up by your contractors' estimates. It is much easier to negotiate a number based on solid facts than one you just made up. Your seller is much more likely to concede to a logical and provable number.

PROPERTY IS TOO EXPENSIVE

If a seller has paid too much for a property, then an MLO might be a good place to start negotiating the deal. Again, you need to know your market well for an MLO. If your city has rapidly increasing values in the type of property you are trying to obtain, you'll want to get a long term on the MLO so that in the years to come, the value will rise and surpass the payoff amount of the property. Use the high payoff to negotiate a longer term for the MLO. During your negotiation, you want to let the seller know that the property price does not meet the current market value (use sales comps to support this).

You also want to know at what rate your market is appreciating. You can get this data from local realtors. Use these figures to decide how long it will take for the value of the property to rise above the current payoff amount. This is how long you'll want to have the MLO in place. You can apply the same concept if you are getting seller financing on a property. The seller needs to hold financing long enough for the market to catch up with the price. Use provable statistics to support this time frame in your negotiations.

EXISTING MORTGAGE

I have already discussed the situation of having a seller finance a deal to you that already has a mortgage in place. If you find this type of deal, then you can negotiate little or no down payment. If the seller requires money from you to get into the deal, then negotiate an MLO offer.

LOW OCCUPANCY, BAD MANAGEMENT, OR LITTLE TO NO CASH FLOW

These are all areas in which you can negotiate good terms for CSF. You'll want to negotiate heavily on the terms of the financing you receive.

When negotiating a CSF, remember to give on price and take on terms. You may want to make your offer closer to the seller's asking price, but ask for terms that make the deal operate better than before. You don't want to pay too much, but you may have to pay a little more to attract the seller to the offer. If this is the case, make sure you set up the terms of the agreement so the deal makes sense from an operational and cash flow standpoint.

You might ask for these terms:

1. Interest-only payments
2. No payments for several months in the beginning of the agreement
3. Lower payments (more cash flow for you)
4. Longer amortization terms if you are doing seller financing
5. Lower interest rates
6. Longer term for the agreement

The terms of your agreement will dramatically affect the operations of your deal, so pay close attention to them when you are negotiating the finer points of your agreement. You should negotiate the terms to create as much cash flow with as little risk as possible.

NEGOTIATING IN REAL ESTATE DEALS

Data gathering is arguably the most important aspect of any good negotiation. Without knowing what will motivate the other side, you are flying blind. Once you gather all the applicable information you can, it's time to make the offer. When you create your offer, make it reasonable for them at first glance, but also make it great for you.

The seller will likely push back on some of the terms or the price you are offering. At this point in the negotiation, you'll discuss the plan you have for the property. Discuss the distress issues of the property and how your offer will allow you to solve these problems. Now that you've made your general sales pitch to the seller, you can start discussing the finer points of the deal. This is where your skills as a negotiator will come into play.

PRINCIPLED NEGOTIATION

Principled negotiation is described in the well-known book *Getting to Yes*, written by Roger Fisher and William Ury, first published in 1981. One facet of this technique is the use of a mutually accepted principle in which there are set standards for the negation.

Here's a real estate example of principled negotiation: If I want to buy a house, the seller may ask for $500,000. You may want to pay only $400,000 for the house. So to find a mutually accepted principle, you need a third-party valuation for the house. A market standard for this valuation is comparable sales prices of similar properties in the area. If you and the seller agree that comparable sales are a fair measure for value in that market, then you have a standard for value and can negotiate from there.

Here is another example: If I use my contractors to give me estimates for repairs needed to your property and I want to use them to negotiate the down payment, the seller may not agree to using my contractors. They may want to use their contractors instead. In this case, we may need to get three bids—two from our contractors and one from a contractor we find in the phone book. Then we can find a standard, or "principle."

Whenever you start to make offers for a CSF, always look for a "principle" to support your offer. This will take the pressure off you and put it onto a third party helping to establish a value.

PRINCIPLED NEGOTIATION IN ACTION

Someone at a real estate conference once asked me about negotiating a time frame for seller financing. The person told me they had made an offer for seller financing and it had been accepted by the seller, but the negotiation broke down over the financing time frame. The seller wanted to give financing for only 1 year, and the buyer knew the deal would take longer than that to complete. This was for a larger apartment complex that was a distressed asset.

My advice to this buyer was to use principled negotiation to overcome the stalemate in the negotiation. The property needed a fair number of repairs as well as stabilized occupancy. The buyer's plan was to refinance the deal with a traditional lender after the property had been stabilized, therefore paying off the seller's financing. This buyer needed third-party criteria to give validity to his request for the loan time. Otherwise, it was simply a battle of "wants," and he was losing.

I told this guy to go to his contractors and get estimates for the time it would take to complete the repairs. Then he needed to ask some local managers how long it would take to lease the vacant units in his market. Last, he needed to talk to some of the lenders he wanted to refinance the deal with. It was likely the lenders would want him to own the property for a certain period before they'd even consider refinancing the deal (seasoning period). Typically, the seasoning period is about 12–18 months, but this depends on the lender and the financial strength of the borrower.

After he gathered these time frames, he could add them together and present this data to the seller to help negotiate a longer time for his loan. This way, it was not simply the buyer asking for something he wanted and the seller not wanting to give it. Now he had legitimate data that supported the longer time frame. The data supported his argument.

You will find many ways to apply principled negotiation in each deal, and each deal will be totally different from the last.

GENERAL TIPS

The following are some general tips and techniques for negotiating. These can be applied to all negotiations.

➤ Attitude is everything when solving someone's problems. If you're going to make a problem-solving offer, you need to be confident in yourself but not arrogant. If I have a problem and you tell me you can solve it but you are nervous or unsure, I won't believe you. If I have a problem, I need a problem-solving hero. Be a hero!

➤ Always be ready to walk away. This is what I call doorknob negotiation. I am your problem-solving hero, and if you don't see that or agree, then I'm willing to walk away, leave you with your problems, and go solve someone else's problems. When negotiations break down, get up and leave. About the time your hand hits the doorknob, the seller will agree and get down to business, or they will let you leave. Either way, you have a solid answer.

➤ Do most of your negotiating before you create a contract. When you get a contract, try your best to honor the deal you have agreed upon. There's a time to negotiate and there is a time to perform; know the difference.

➤ Deadlines are a powerful negotiating tool. If you have a deadline, it can make you weak. If the seller has a deadline, you can leverage that to your advantage. If the seller must close by a certain time or has some other type of deadline, it can work in your favor. Strategically, push negotiations as close to the deadline as you ethically can. 80 percent of concessions are given in the last 20 percent of time before a deadline. Run the clock out and then play hard.

➤ The tradeoff: When someone asks you for something, always ask for something in return. If you don't, they will keep asking for more and more until you put your foot down. Everyone with children understands this one. Don't give concessions for free.

> The nibble: Keep asking for something until the other side puts their foot down. You can get a ton of concessions from a seller before they catch on and start using the tradeoff.

> Red herring: This is a common term meaning "something useless." I will often put something into an offer I don't really care about at all. It's usually something I know the seller won't agree with. I will act as if this red herring is very important to me, and when the seller moves to strike that from the offer, I go into the tradeoff technique by saying, "Well, if I have to give that up, then I want this instead." The thing I'm asking for in the trade is something I *do* want.

You'll want to use a combination of these techniques in your negotiations. If the seller has a deadline, then you may put in a red herring saying you want a bunch of repairs before closing. When the seller says no to that, you can say you can't close by the deadline date. When they get upset about that, you could give the concession of closing by the time they want, but you need some money off the asking price in return. By using the deadline, red herring, and tradeoff in the negotiation, you can get the price reduced.

Negotiating is not a win-or-lose situation, and to believe so will make you weak in your efforts. A good negotiator will solve everyone's problems, not just their own. If you make doing business with you profitable, you'll have more business than you know what to do with. Ask for what you want; negotiate for what you need.

NEGOTIATING A MASTER LEASE OPTION

Negotiating the MLO begins long before the offer is made. All good negotiations begin with gathering information, and it's no different with an MLO. The first bit of information you gather will help you determine the motivation of the seller. If a property is a distressed asset (low occupancy, deferred maintenance, etc.), the seller is more likely to be motivated to sell the property. If a property is a money maker, the seller is less likely to be motivated to sell.

Not all motivated sellers are motivated because the property isn't making money, but most are. Take a close look at the property itself. If you find, in your first analysis, that the property is distressed or the seller is motivated for other reasons, then this is a prime situation for an MLO. As I stated in the realtor section, do not approach a seller or agent and directly ask for an MLO deal. This can make it seem like you have no money.

A good negotiation will be based on your ability to make the seller see the big picture. You need to make the seller aware they have a problem without rubbing their nose in it. Create an objective situation with which to leverage your position. You will do this with your analysis of the deal. Gather all the financial data you can and calculate the cash flow or lack thereof. Gather all the data you can about repairs needed for the property, including the approximate cost of repairs. Calculate the value of the deal using the income approach.

You want to understand the value of a deal and be able to gently educate your seller on the value. Most sellers have an unrealistic view of their property's worth. Your job is to bring their value back in line with reality and, at the same time, get them to realize the MLO is the solution to the problem.

Once you calculate the property's value, you have its worth derived through logic and the property's income. Your offer and valuation will be based on numbers that are logical and explainable. Otherwise, the seller may feel you are making a lowball offer just to steal a deal. Once you have an objective value for the property, make the seller aware of a few things:

1. A lack of cash flow will not allow the property to qualify for a bank loan.
2. If the property will not qualify for a bank loan, then the seller is looking for an all-cash offer.
3. If the seller gets a cash offer, it is likely to be about half of what the asking price is because it's all cash.
4. If a buyer (besides you) were to come to this market with cash, would they buy something distressed, or would they leverage their money and buy something that is currently operational? Make the seller realize that all buyers will approach the asset the same way as you.

You also need the seller to understand that you did not create this problem, but you are willing to help them solve it. This is where the offer for an MLO comes in. You can gently make the seller realize the magnitude of the situation and then suggest the master lease as a possible solution to the deal. This takes time, but if you don't spend time getting your seller to this point, your MLO offer may be misunderstood. *Remember, a confused mind says no.*

Now you must put on your sales hat and get ready to sell! After all of this negotiation, all you are selling is yourself.

You'll need to convince the seller that the MLO is a way to solve their problems and you are the person for the job. Also, keep in mind that sellers may not admit that they don't know how MLOs work. If you think they don't, then your job will be to explain how it works without making them feel stupid.

POINTS TO REMEMBER

Negotiation is an art that takes time and practice. Start practicing now!

Not everyone knows when they have a problem. This is never truer than in real estate. Sometimes owners have no idea how distressed their asset really is or how overpriced it may be. It's your job through the negotiation process to identify the issues with any asset and strategically bring them up with the seller. Just because the seller doesn't realize they have a problem doesn't mean it's not there. It just means they'll *act* like they don't.

Use the negotiation process to identify the seller's motivations and offer equitable solutions. If a seller doesn't feel they are getting a fair deal, they might not move forward with you.

Don't replace creativity with compromise. Instead of creating an offer that creates a mid-level compromise, think creatively and make an offer that gives each side more than they expected. That's a great negotiation.

ACTION ITEMS

Take your negotiation education to the next level. Start reading and studying everything you can on the subject. Here are three works to start with:

1. *Getting to Yes* by Roger Fisher and William Ury
2. *Never Split the Difference* by Chris Voss
3. *Negotiate This* by Herb Cohen

CHAPTER 13

EXIT STRATEGIES

Know the way out...before you get in! A good investor/business owner always has a solid exit strategy before they get into a deal. Ideally, you should have several exit strategies.

Closing on a property is not the key in real estate. Getting out profitably is! Many people have gone into foreclosure or bankruptcy in past market cycles. Those people didn't have trouble getting into deals—they had trouble getting out financially intact.

The following are some exit strategies for creative financing deals.

REFINANCING

This is one of my favorite exit strategies. It can also be one of the most difficult but creative type of financing, as many possibilities are open for this exit.

Typically, to refinance with a traditional lender, the property must no longer be a distressed asset. This means the repairs need to be complete. If it's multifamily, then the property needs to be stabilized. Most lenders want to see 90 for 90, meaning the occupancy needs to be over 90 percent for at least 90 days. This will get you the best terms with most lenders. This is the beauty of CSF. The financing you get from the seller allows you to take over the operations of the property and make the necessary adjustments to make it profitable (exactly how the lenders like them).

If refinancing is an exit strategy you want to use, there are several things you will do. Get in touch with at least three lenders and get verbal approval for the refinance before you take passion with CSF. I say "verbal" because you can't get any other kind of approval unless you are in an actual application process. What you are trying to do is find three lenders that like the deal and feel they would refinance the property once you complete all the repairs.

Show the lenders your plans for the project. Show them the purchase price and the amount of money you plan to spend on fixing it up. Show the occupancy and your plans for management. You want to have a feel for the lending market and which lenders will have an appetite for refinancing the project before you get into a CSF contract.

When planning to refinance a property, don't forget the "seasoning period." This is the length of time a traditional lender wants you to own the property. Ask about this when you first contact the lenders. You want to make sure the length of the CSF agreement gives you ample time to season the ownership. This creates a seamless transition into traditional lending.

REFINANCING IN ACTION

In late 2008 to early 2009, I bought seven houses with money I borrowed from a private lender. I had been purchasing houses with the backing of this private money for a while. I would close on several houses, and once I had a pack of them, I refinanced with my local bank. It was going well until the credit market crashed. It crashed while I had the seven houses I paid for with private money. I had planned on refinancing quickly, but it didn't happen. I went past my loan due date and couldn't pay the lender back. I was in a foreclosure situation.

The lender was good to me and didn't foreclose. He did, however, charge me a small fortune to continue the loan! Many months and a ton of high-interest payments later, I qualified for bank financing and paid the private lender back. This is why you need to know your exit strategy when going into a deal. If refinancing is your preference, then get to know your bankers before you close with CSF. This will increase the chances of a successful exit and keep you from making the same mistake I did.

FLIP OR WHOLESALE

Creative financing is a great tool for people who plan to flip or wholesale properties. If you can secure a great price for a property and control it with CSF, then you've bought yourself some time to go out and find a buyer. Be sure to include any of your down payment money and rehab costs into the price of the loan, but don't get too greedy. Being greedy is one of the most expensive habits you can have.

If you are trying to make some quick cash by selling a property you just took control of, you'll want to leave some value in the deal for the next person. Keep in mind they may need to qualify for a loan to be able to purchase it from you. They'll want to feel they are getting a good deal, too. They'll have to deal with the same lending parameters and time frames that you did, so allow for this in the terms the seller gives you when you first set up your CSF agreement.

Tip: The most successful wholesalers and flippers I have ever known were great because they had an exceptionally large list of buyers before they went into a deal. You should always be building your list of buyers. That way, when you get a deal under a CSF agreement, you can quickly call your list of buyers and sell for some fast cash!

MASTER LEASE OPTION ASSIGNMENT

If you are doing an MLO, then you have a tradable item. A master lease can be assigned to someone else if your attorney sets the document up correctly. A person would buy a master lease from you to collect the income stream created by the property. Keep this in mind when you originally set up the agreement.

You can also sell the option to purchase if you have kept the documents separate. You can keep the master lease that allows you to control the property and sell the option to purchase to someone else. This gives them the right to purchase the property for the price you previously negotiated.

The MLO is a great addition to a wholesaling strategy. Wholesaling is when you put a property under contract and then assign the contract to another buyer for a fee. The point of wholesaling is controlling the property with a contract for a short amount of time while you find a buyer to purchase that control from you for a fee.

An MLO assignment is not much different and can follow a similar strategy. Once you take control of a property with an MLO, you will then have time to market the property and find a buyer. You can draft your MLO contract to be assignable. If the seller agrees for the contract to be assignable, then you can sell your option interest to someone else for a lump sum of cash. Have your attorney draft the agreement to be assignable.

HOLD AND OPERATE

This is a great long-term exit strategy. If you can get CSF for long enough to hold and operate, great! If not, then refinance the deal and operate it under the new financing.

I mentioned talking to lenders before closing with the CSF. Here is another reason to do so. If you know the general terms in which you'd refinance the deal before you take control, then you know what terms and price to set up with your CSF. Traditional lending should have a longer term and less interest than the CSF. Once you get the loan in place, you can hold and operate the property even more profitably than before.

Regardless of what your long-term exit strategy is, if you plan to hold and operate the property for any length of time, make sure the term of any loan allows you to cash flow. As mentioned in the beginning of this chapter, whatever exit strategy you plan to employ, you need to know what it is before you get into the deal.

EXIT STRATEGIES FOR THE MASTER LEASE OPTION DEAL

To reemphasize, if you cannot execute a successful exit strategy, you will find yourself in trouble. A successful exit strategy should be created long before you sign on the dotted line. If you cannot conceive of several reasonable exit strategies in your deal analysis, then you may not be looking at a good deal. Let's look at some exit strategies specific to MLO deals.

SELL THE LEASE

In this case, you will sell the lease but retain the option rights separately. The purchase of the lease purchases the rights stated in your lease, such as profits above the lease payments. People will purchase the lease to buy the income stream. If this is an exit strategy you plan to use, try to get the longest possible lease term. This will increase the salability of the lease.

SURRENDER THE MASTER LEASE OPTION

In short, this means that during the MLO term, you decide the property is not worth buying and you walk away from the deal, forfeiting the option money. This would be a worst-case scenario, but if you realize the deal won't hold its value, it may be smarter to lose the option money or whatever portion you have not yet earned back in cash flow. You don't want to close on a bad deal that may continue to lose money.

CLOSE THE OPTION

In this exit strategy, you exercise your option to purchase and close the deal. If you have cash on hand to purchase the property, then you'll simply close with an attorney and take possession of the property like a regular sale. If you don't have the cash at closing, then you can refinance the deal.

REFINANCE

Refinancing is not an optional exit for an MLO deal. You are a renter, not an owner. You cannot refinance something you don't own. When you exercise your option to purchase, the lender will consider it a new purchase. Typically, the lender will lend on the appraisal for the asset or the purchase price (option price in the MLO), whichever is lower.

You're likely to be given experiential credit for having operated the asset during your hold time, but this likely won't affect the loan amount. You should be prepared to bring an applicable amount of down payment money to the deal if you plan to exercise the options by using traditional debt.

GIVE SOMEONE ELSE A MASTER LEASE OPTION

Some people have properties they wish they didn't have. I started my real estate career buying houses. I still have some of those houses today, and I wish I didn't. If you ever find yourself in this situation, you can give someone else an MLO. You can reverse everything I have taught you in this book and be on the other side of the equation.

If you have a property that is not currently making money—maybe you don't want to manage it or it needs to be fixed up to be rentable again—an MLO could be your solution. All you need to do is recruit a buyer for your deal. Since you are the one with the MLO education, you may need to educate your buyer. You'll want to be careful and screen your buyer the same way you would screen a seller. Find someone with the time and energy to get your distressed asset back into good shape. Here are a few things I suggest:

1. Be willing to give an amount of free rent equal to the repair costs. If the rent is $500 per month with $2,000 in repairs, give the buyer 4 months of free rent to get the repairs done. Then they should be making payments to you.
2. Make the buyer use their option money to do repairs. Ask them to put it into an escrow account where you can see it.
3. Don't give a master lease for longer than your loan term.
4. Make the monthly payment equal to your mortgage payment, plus a percentage of the profits.
5. Have the buyer escrow for taxes, insurance, and mortgage payment.

In the summer of 2016, I used this "exit strategy" with a four-unit property I had in a marginal neighborhood. It became difficult to collect rent there, and the tenants became difficult to deal with. The rents in this building were low, and I came to the conclusion that I was losing money by dealing with this property. A better use of my time would be to focus on managing several hundred units that did make money or getting another property that cash flowed a few hundred bucks a month. The decision to "exit" became a no-brainer!

Once I realized the opportunity cost of dealing with this quad, I decided to give an MLO to a local church. They had no idea how a master lease worked, so I explained it. They were more than eager to take control of the property for me. I gave them several months of free rent in exchange for doing the repairs. Their payment to me covered the mortgage, taxes, and insurance amounts. I let them have the property at break-even. It no longer makes me any profit, but it breaks even. I keep the tax benefits of ownership, and I can make money running other more profitable properties.

The church loves it. They don't care about making it cash flow because they use the units for a battered women's program. We all win!

Use the MLO exit strategy to solve your distressed asset problems. You could start with churches, nonprofits, and new investors. Give someone a break in the business, and it solves your headaches, too.

POINTS TO REMEMBER

Know the way out before you go in. The exit strategy is the first aspect to consider in any deal analysis.

I hate the comment "You make money when you buy." I think this is one of the most dangerous and limited points of view in the real estate business. You may *create value* when you buy, but you only *make money* when you exit the deal profitably. Ask anyone who has lost a deal in foreclosure if they made money when they bought the property.

"You make money when you buy" means you are guaranteed to make money if you just close a deal. NOT TRUE! This mindset completely devalues the importance of an exit strategy. If you do not have a solid exit strategy, how can you know if the plan for your property will work out? Again, know the way out before you go in.

ACTION ITEMS

Create three pro forma business plans for three deals. Analyze each deal by beginning with one of these exit strategies. Analyze all three deals with all suggested exits and see what you get.

1. Refinance in 3 years (or less)
   A. Will the value increase enough in 3 years or less?
2. Sell in 4–5 years
   A. What market cycle will you be in then?
3. MLO for 3 years
   A. What is the exit strategy after the 3 years?
      i. Buy (exercise the option)?
      ii. Sell?
      iii. Assign the contract for a fee?
4. Seller financing for 3 years
   A. What interest rate will you offer to make the deal work?
   B. How much down payment?

CHAPTER 14

STEP-BY-STEP WALK-THROUGH

The following is a bird's-eye view of a deal, start to finish, for reference. This is simply a bullet list of items to give you a general sense of the deal process and what to look for. You can come back to this chapter for reference and also to find specific topics within the book.

1. Deal flow (chapter 8)
   A. The first step: get deals to analyze
   B. Ways to find deals:
      i. Over fifty units
         a. Realtors are the main source
         b. Go to realtor's website
         c. Find currently listed deals
         d. Analyze and then contact listing agent
      ii. Under fifty units
         a. Go directly to owner
         b. Set up direct contact campaign (call, text, email, etc.)
         c. Network for owners/sellers
2. Deal analysis (chapter 9)
   A. Real money is made on the spread sheet.

B. Begin with exit strategy:
   i. How long should you hold the asset?
   ii. What market cycle are you in now, and what cycle will you be in when you exit?
C. Is the asset distressed?
   i. If yes:
      a. Why?
      b. How?
      c. What will it take to fix the deal?
      d. How long?
      e. How much cash?
   ii. If no:
      a. Is the seller motivated to sell for some personal reason?
      b. Is the seller motivated by the market conditions?
D. What types of CSF could you use to "fix" the deal?
3. Make the offer (chapter 10)
   A. SPY
   B. Solve problems
   C. Creativity before compromise
   D. Use an LOI
4. Negotiate the offer (chapter 12)
   A. The LOI is used to negotiate the major terms of the deal.
   B. Give on price, take on terms.
      i. Most sellers are more motivated by the overall price of a deal than the terms of the CSF.
      ii. Be flexible on the price, but negotiate terms that allow you to control and stabilize the asset.
         a. Interest-only
         b. No down payment
         c. Low interest rate

    C. Have an attorney negotiate and create any binding legal documents. (Don't cut and paste from the internet.)

5. Do your due diligence (chapter 10)
    A. Conduct due diligence as if you were buying the deal with your grandmother's life savings.
    B. Walk all units.
    C. Do full financial and lease audits.
    D. Remember, just because you *can* do a CSF deal does not mean you *should*.

6. Close (chapter 10)
    A. Use a title company or legal counsel to close the transaction.
    B. Make sure your CSF documents are legally recorded to protect your interest in the deal.

7. Take over operations (chapter 7)
    A. Hire management.
    B. Become your own management company.

8. Exit the deal (chapter 13)
    A. Sell
    B. Keep the asset and refinance (pull cash out)
    C. Give creative financing
    D. Repeat steps 1–8

DUE DILIGENCE CHECKLIST

Obtain complete copies of the following documents to the extent such documents are in the seller's or seller's property manager's possession or reasonable control:

1. Current rent roll and access to all tenant files (on-site) and all leases, as well as copies of all laundry leases and other commercial leases

2. All existing American Land Title Association (ALTA) surveys, seller's existing title policy and underlying documents
3. Lease activity report for the past 60 days
4. Property brochure including property logo, floor plans, and site plan
5. List of personal property inventory
6. Property tax bills for the period of seller's ownership
7. Capital expenditure summary and list of site improvements for the period of seller's ownership
8. Standard lease agreement and addenda forms
9. Copies of all service contracts and a vendor summary
10. Copies of all existing permits, certificates, and licenses
11. Utility provider list, including all current providers, and utility invoices and billing information for the period of seller's ownership
12. All Phase 1 Environmental Reports and any other environmental reports or studies regarding the property
13. Year-to-date statement of income and expenses for the latest month available and for the period of seller's ownership
14. Most current engineering reports and any third-party reports regarding the condition of the property, including, without limitation, soils reports, structural reports, roof reports, HVAC reports, structural calculations and seismic reports, parking lot reports, pest control/termite reports (including inspection and treatment reports), engineering reports, Americans with Disabilities Act compliance surveys, fire sprinkler reports, elevator reports, and similar reports or studies with respect to the property
15. As-built plans and specifications relating to the original development of the property, renovation, and any major capital repairs

16. Maintenance records for the period of seller's ownership, including year-to-date and maintenance requests/log, past 12 months' work-order history by unit number, completion dates, and all pending maintenance requests

17. Copies of notices of violations of any federal, state, municipal, or other health, fire, building, zoning, safety, environmental protection, or other applicable codes, laws, rules, regulations, or ordinances relating or applying to the property, if any

18. Insurance loss runs for the period of seller's ownership (including _____ year-to-date)

19. An operational budget, including revenue projections for the property for calendar year _____.

20. Monthly profit and loss statements for the period of seller's ownership; through the effective date _____.

21. A schedule of all pending or threatened litigation or governmental proceedings or enforcement actions relating to or affecting the leases or the property and known to seller

22. All warranties, guarantees, and indemnities made by or received from any third party with respect to any part of the property and known to seller

23. The most current zoning report for the property

CONCLUSION

Business has been founded on one concept since the beginning of our societies: cooperation. If you can get others to cooperate with you, you do not need cash. The fastest way to get someone to cooperate with you is to solve their problems.

Many sellers of real estate assets have problems. Some of them know it, and some do not. It's your job to identify sellers who have problems you can solve and to make creative offers that communicate this.

Always have something to trade. If you don't bring any value to a seller, you are unlikely to be successful with a creative offer. Find your value and trade for it. Perhaps it's just time and energy that you bring, but if you look hard enough, you will find a seller who needs just that and is willing to trade. The techniques in this book will help you create value for a seller through creative strategies and problem-solving offers.

Creativity takes practice. Be ready to get out and make some offers. Be ready to get rejected. This is normal and good. The real offer process can't begin until someone says no. Get to the no as fast as you can. Hearing no from a seller is not a failure. It's the beginning of the negotiation. Be patient with yourself. Success takes time.

Continuing education is key. It doesn't matter if you are starting out in the real estate business or if you are a veteran of many market cycles—you always have more to learn.

I've joined with Jake and Gino in creating a lot of real estate education material. I don't need to teach; I do it because I enjoy it. I wouldn't work with these two guys if they didn't share the same values for education that I have. For more info and videos, check out www.creativeapartmentdeals. com.

Good luck out there!

Bill Ham

MORE FROM JAKE & GINO PUBLISHING

THE HONEY BEE

A business parable that teaches the value of cultivating multiple streams of income, *The Honey Bee* tells the story of Noah, a disappointed, disaffected salesman who feels like his life is going nowhere until he has a chance encounter with a man named Tom Barnham, a beekeeper. In his charming, down-home way and using the lessons he's learned from his beekeeping passion, Tom the "Bee Man" teaches Noah and his wife, Emma, how to grow their personal wealth.

For more information, visit www.jakeandgino.com/honeybee.

LEARN MORE FROM JAKE & GINO AND BECOME SUCCESSFUL IN YOUR REAL ESTATE BUSINESS TODAY

If you've enjoyed this book, we hope you will take a moment to check out the additional resources we offer at www.jakeandgino.com.

Jake & Gino is a multifamily community created to teach investors how to become multifamily entrepreneurs by engaging with members and providing weekly podcasts, blogs, and training videos.

To begin your journey with Jake & Gino, visit www.jakeandgino.com.

Bill Ham has created a separate website with additional resources that correspond with the teachings in this book.

Visit www.creativeapartmentdeals.com for access to videos and downloads to help you in your real estate journey.

ABOUT THE AUTHOR

Jake Stenziano, Bill Ham, and Gino Barbaro

BILL HAM

Bill Ham, formerly a commercial pilot, left the corporate aviation life and started Phoenix Residential Group with a duplex and a dream. More than 15 years later, he's built a portfolio of over 1,000 units and has been involved in the analysis and operations of thousands more.

Bill's first 400 units were purchased without stepping foot into a bank. He's used the creative financing options he shares in this book to secure his first 400 units under management.

He is also a Deal Expert Coach with the Jake & Gino team, where he mentors students who are looking to create and grow a multifamily portfolio for themselves and their families.

JAKE STENZIANO AND GINO BARBARO

Jake Stenziano and Gino Barbaro are best-selling authors of *Wheelbarrow Profits* and *The Honey Bee*. They are also the founders of Jake & Gino, an educational platform helping others to achieve financial freedom through multifamily real estate investing.

Jake and Gino have built a portfolio of over 1,600 multifamily units and host *Wheelbarrow Profits*, one of the top multifamily real estate podcasts on iTunes.